HUMATA · HUKHTA · HVARSHTA

THE HEARTBEAT OF A TRUST

*The success of his life was mainly due to
the singleness of purpose with which he
devoted himself to the development of
Indian industries and to the promotion of
the great industrial schemes conceived by
his father.*

*Sir Dorabji's fame, however, will not rest on his
great achievements, splendid as they were,
or on his wealth, but it will rest solidly
on the use he has made of his possessions.*

—The Times of India
June 4, 1932
on the occasion of the death of
Sir Dorabji Tata

Dedicated
to the memory of
Prof. R.D. Choksi
who wrote a good part of this story
in deeds
which I have tried to recapture only in words

THE HEARTBEAT

OF

A TRUST

The Story of Sir Dorabji Tata Trust

by
R.M. LALA

Illustrated by
Mario Miranda

With a Foreword by
J.R.D. Tata

TATA McGRAW-HILL PUBLISHING COMPANY LIMITED
NEW DELHI

McGraw-Hill Offices
New Delhi   New York   St. Louis   San Francisco   Auckland   Bogota
Caracas   Lisbon   London   Madrid   Mexico City   Milan   Montreal
San Juan   Singapore   Sydney   Tokyo   Toronto

Tata McGraw-Hill
A Division of The McGraw-Hill Companies

First Edition: March 1984
Second Edition: June 1984
Revised Third Edition: 1998

This edition can be exported from India only by the publishers, Tata McGraw-Hill Publishing Company Limited

ISBN: 0-07-463246-9

Published by Tata McGraw-Hill Publishing Company Limited, 7 West Patel Nagar, New Delhi 110 008, and printed by Mr. A.S. Vadiwala, Tata Donnelley Limited, 414 Veer Savarkar Marg, Mumbai 400 025

One way to take injustice out of riches is to dedicate riches to the service of the people and of the nation. The entire possessions of Sir Dorabji Tata were placed in a trust. They included shares, landed estates and jewellery valued in all at Rs. 1 crore* in 1932, the equivalent of Rs. 83.4 crores of 1997. It included the 245-carat Jubilee Diamond, twice as large as the Koh-i-noor.

A diamond in a bank vault is just a diamond. Sold, and its proceeds intelligently harnessed, it can enrich the lives of thousands.

This is the story of a foundation and of the men and women who used its funds to pioneer for India the study of social sciences; of fundamental sciences; the treatment of and research in cancer; integrated rural development; and, more recently, preservation of the country's rich heritage of the performing arts.

The wealth garnered by Sir Dorabji Tata established the institution that built the first atomic reactor in Asia. It also sent hundreds for higher studies abroad, including a blind Indian, who by a miracle of modern science, out of darkness, found sight.

---

* A crore is Rs. 10 million; and a lakh is Rs. 100,000.

The author is grateful to a number of people for getting the copy ready for the press.

Ms. Khorshed Divecha for casting her professional eye over the manuscript.

Mrs. Villoo Karkaria for coordination of the manuscript and Mr. Saby Mathias for typing

Mr. Mohammad Ibrahim for DTP layout.

The staff of Tata McGraw-Hill for publishing and of Tata Donnelley Limited for printing the book.

Contents

VI Other Ventures

VII In the Lives of the People

Foreword

I am happy to respond to Russi Lala's invitation to write a Foreword to his book on fifty years* of the Sir Dorabji Tata Trust, because that story of half a century of service to the people needed to be told for historical and archival purposes as well as for guidance to other donors. I am especially happy that the story has been written by Russi Lala for no one could have done a better or more scholarly job of the task, which has fully benefited from his rare and felicitous ability to write simple, honest and lucid English.

Many Trusts do good work but their activities may not necessarily make good reading. The Dorabji Tata Trust has the material for a readable book and the author has told it in an unconventional way. He has written it not as a documentary history but as a story of people who have shaped it and of some who have benefited from it. As he says in the Preface he has tried to 'highlight the human endeavours that has enabled the Trust to reach into the sensitive spheres of national life.' The personalities whose pen sketches he has drawn include Dr. Clifford Manshardt, the American social scientist, Prof. R.D. Choksi and Dr. Homi Bhabha, whose personality is still felt in the corridors of the institution he founded.

Though Sir Dorabji's Trust is the premier Foundation of Tatas today, the tradition of Tata philanthropy was set by Jamsetji, the Founder of the House. The grand vision was his. To his sons, Dorabji and Ratan, and his cousin, R.D. Tata, goes the credit of continuing the tradition.

The word 'philanthropy' has a more profound meaning than that of mere charity for its derivative is *fil-anthra-pi* which means 'love of mankind'. When that love prevails,

---

* This Foreword was written in 1984 for the first edition of this book now revised and updated till 1996, covering 64 years of the Trust.

wealth assumes a nobler purpose. Jamsetji lived in an age when philanthropy was its own reward; tax benefits not being an added attraction then!

In his Preface the author has brought out the fact that Jamsetji was exercised about the use of wealth at the same time as Carnegie and Rockefeller, though Jamsetji's wealth was on a much smaller scale. Rockefeller and Carnegie had the advantage of operating within a climate of freedom. They lived in a rapidly developing industrial society. Jamsetji had to operate within a climate of servitude, in a primarily agricultural country, whose age-old industries were drained by foreign rulers to provide a market for exports of the Imperial power. It was in such a setting that Jamsetji arrived on the Indian scene. He was a man sensitive to the suffering of his people but realised that 'patchwork philanthropy' as he called it—giving some food here and clothes there—would not go far. So he formulated his philosophy of 'constructive philanthropy'. He defined it thus: 'What advances a nation or a community is not so much to prop up its weakest and most helpless members but to lift up the best and the most gifted, so as to make them of the greatest service to the country'. With this end in view he launched the J.N. Tata Endowment Scheme for Higher Education in 1892 sending abroad future administrators, scientists, doctors, lawyers and engineers; and he formulated his major scheme of a University of Science (and Technology) to give India the technological personnel that would enable it to step into the industrial age.

Jamsetji died seven years before the Indian Institute of Science opened at Bangalore. The author reveals that Sir Dorabji, in fact, made an offer as large as Jamsetji's to the Institute of Science for an Institute of Tropical Medicine to be a part of the institution his father endowed. But Dr. Ramsay, the Director of the Institute, declined the gift as he feared that it was too much for his fledgling institution to cope with.

The task of the Trustees of a philanthropic foundation in

a country like India is more onerous than in a more affluent society. Faced with the magnitude of the needs and sufferings of a vast population, the Trustees are torn between the urge, on the one hand, to respond to immediate needs and, on the other, taking a long-term view, to plant the seeds out of which will grow the trees that will yield rich fruit for generations to come. While they did not neglect pressing immediate demands, the Trustees decided that the main thrust of their policies would be aimed at long-term and self-generating benefits, and particularly recognised the vital importance of education in promoting economic growth and raising standards of life. As a result, educational grants constitute about 60 per cent of the total annual disbursements of the Trust.

The Trustees also made the significant decision that, apart from extending support to existing institutions with priority given to education, the Trust should from time to time, funds permitting, promote on its own projects of an innovative and pioneering nature which did not exist in the country and which would not have come to birth otherwise. Thus came to life the Tata Memorial Hospital for Cancer Research and Treatment, the Tata Institute of Fundamental Research, the Tata Institute of Social Sciences and last, but certainly not the least, the National Centre for the Performing Arts. Of the total funds disbursed by the Trust in these 50 years, about half was devoted to such sponsored projects both in their establishment and for their running expenditure.

The Tata Memorial Hospital was one of the first of these projects, for the creation and running of which the Trust was almost wholly responsible until 1957. Later the Trust made a gift of it to the nation. I took a special interest in the building of the Hospital and made somewhat of a nuisance of myself with the architects who did not always satisfy functional and aesthetic requirements which were not, I must confess, always wholly compatible.

In the fifty years of endeavour in which I was privileged to be associated with the Trust and felt deeply involved in it, my own contribution was a modest one. It was Professor Rustum Choksi who provided the leadership, generated the ideas and set the tone of the Sir Dorabji Tata Trust.

As I look back upon these fifty years, I realise that, in the context of the immensity of the needs of the people, our contribution has inevitably been a quantitatively small one. I hope, however, that the readers of Russi Lala's splendid book will conclude that it was qualitatively significant, and that in handling the wealth placed in our hands we fulfilled the vision and aims of Jamsetji Tata and his sons that this wealth which came from the people should go back to the people many times over.

Bombay, January 9, 1984

Preface

$\mathbf{M}$y earlier book, *The Creation of Wealth*,[1] looked into the Tata story primarily from the angle of the generation of wealth for the nation. People are also interested in knowing how the considerable funds generated by this House are utilised. What, if anything, has it achieved?

The present work takes a look at the activities of this Foundation and its ripple effects on the country.

Trusts or foundations of this type are a twentieth century phenomenon. The first major American foundations were the General Education Board established by John D. Rockefeller in 1902, followed by the Carnegie Foundation for the Advancement of Teaching in 1911. The Rockefeller Foundation was established in 1913. The major British foundations followed with the Leverhulme Trust Fund being established in 1925 and the Nuffield Foundation as late as 1943. A foundation is defined by *The Foundation Directory* [2] as 'a non-governmental, non-profit organisation having a principal fund of its own, managed by its own trustees or directors, and established to maintain or aid social, educational, charitable, religious, or other activities serving the common welfare.'

In the *International Foundation Directory*,[3] H.V. Hodson lays down the following distinguishing characteristics of a foundation:

> The purpose must be recognised as charitable (or 'For the public benefit', to borrow a phrase often used in European legislation) in national law, whether the law is statutory or customary.
>
> It must possess substantial capital assets. It excludes bodies which serve charitable ends by raising money from year to year and spending it as they raise it.

---

1 *The Creation of Wealth—The Tata Story*, India Book House, Bombay 1981 and 1992.
2 Russel Sage Foundation, New York, 1960.
3 Europa Publications, London, 1974.

It must have discretion in the allocation of its money. ... This excludes, as is intended, trusts and funds exclusively for the benefit of particular causes such as named hospitals, schools or colleges.

Conversely, it must not be an organ (subordinate or exclusively linked) of some other institution falling into a different category; for example, a research institute of a university, or an eleemosynary (almsgiving) fund of a trade union, does not qualify.

The Sir Dorabji Tata Trust was registered on March 11, 1932, and the settlor, Sir Dorabji, died on June 3, the same year. The wealth he turned over to the Trust included substantial shares in Tata Sons, Indian Hotels and allied companies, his landed properties and 21 pieces of jewellery left by his wife, who had predeceased him. Among the jewellery left was the famous Jubilee Diamond. The total benefaction was valued then at Rs. 1 crore which in todays terms would be nearer to Rs. 50 crores.

After a hesitant start that helped to clarify the policy of the Trust, the Trustees felt the Trust should undertake such projects as are too major to be undertaken by individuals and as bear a genuine relevance to national welfare. In the next half a century the Trust established:

India's first institute of social sciences
India's first cancer hospital
India's first institute of fundamental research in mathematics and physics, which became the cradle of India's atomic energy programme
A national centre for the performing arts.

It also launched, 45 years ago, one of the first integrated rural projects. Whether it was the Tata Institute of Social Sciences, the Tata Memorial Hospital (for cancer) or the Tata Institute of Fundamental Research, it was not just a question of establishing a pioneering institution but also of educating a nation in that field of endeavour.

From each of these institutions a torrent of ideas, of learning, of research, has cascaded down the years. It has found expression in the training of two generations of social scientists, cancer specialists, and distinguished scientists, some of whom have made India the fifth most advanced nuclear nation two decades ago. The activities of the major institutions and their out-reach in the nation's life, represent the major part of what I have attempted in this book.

In the last decade it has started the National Institute of Advanced Studies in Bangalore and enabled the Dr. M.S. Swaminathan Research Foundation to start the J.R.D. Tata Centre for Ecotechnology in Madras (now Chennai).

Discoveries, investigations, publications, research papers, are just a fraction of the fall-out of the Trust. What has flowed from this foundation is new life for India's millions and an extension of the frontiers of her knowledge. The wonder is that most of the men who have been its Trustees have been captains of industry—men busy with the cares of business, the pressure of deadlines and decision-making—men like Sir Ardeshir Dalal, Dr. John Matthai, both Directors-in-Charge of Tata Steel, Sir Homi Mody and J.R.D. Tata, Chairman of the Tata Group. J.R.D. Tata has been on the Board of Trustees since its inception in 1932 till his death in 1993. He was its Chairman the last 25 years of his life. The present Chairman is Mr. Ratan N. Tata.

At moments when faint hearts faltered at the immensity of projects like the Tata Memorial Hospital or the National Centre for the Performing Arts, J.R.D. Tata brought his zest and authority to bear in order to push through the projects. This drive that conceived and shaped great institutions was the product of a creative urge and a tenacious determination. In some cases (as with Dr. Homi Bhabha and later on with his brother Jamshed) Tatas prepared the soil and accorded to them facilities to fulfil their vision. In Homi's case it was for the Tata Institute of Fundamental Research; in Jamshed's, for the National Centre for the Performing Arts. In the early years, the Trust also carefully picked and financed doctors and nurses that needed to be trained abroad in cancer treatment and in social sciences, so that they could undergird these specialisations in India. In the case of the National

Centre for the Performing Arts, the contribution of the combined Tata Trusts was matched by that of the Tata group of companies. Non-Tata trusts, companies and individuals contributed an almost equal amount.

The Dorabji Tata Trust established three institutions and, after shaping them for a decade or two, handed them over to the nation. The Union Government has been gracious enough to closely associate the Trust with the running of the institutions it founded. In the case of the Tata Institute of Social Sciences (TISS) and the Tata Institute of Fundamental Research (TIFR), the Chairmen of the Boards have so far been representatives of the Tata Trusts.[4] The Trust is also represented on the Governing Council of the Tata Memorial Hospital, which is now run by the Atomic Energy Commission. The Trust still takes keen interest in these institutions and discussions by this writer with those running them indicated that this continued association has proved beneficial to the institutions.

The National Centre for the Performing Arts (NCPA) is a charitable public trust run by a Council of Members on which the Sir Dorabji Tata Trust is represented, Jamshed Bhabha, Trustee-in-Charge of the NCPA, who succeeded J.R.D. Tata as Chairman.

Government has been wise in preserving the autonomy of the TIFR and the Tata Memorial Hospital which are financed by the Atomic Energy Commission. The Tata Institute of Social Sciences is deemed a university with its own Governing Board on which the Trust, the government and the University Grants Commission are represented. If these institutions are today well run, if they still maintain standards of excellence, the credit goes to the people who run them and the government which, in its wisdom, has allowed them to function with effective independence.

In addition to their four national enterprises and a pioneer

---

4 The Sir Ratan Tata Trust sometimes joined Sir Dorabji Tata Trust with its own contribution as in the case of the Tata Institute of Social Sciences.

rural programme, the Trust started, with the assistance of the Royal Commonwealth Society for the Blind, Asia's first institute for the training of the rural blind; and, with the cooperation of the United Nations, the International Institute of Demographic Studies. The Trust has also undergirded the initiative of several other institutions. Some of these ventures have been covered in the latter part of this book.

What does it take to pioneer great national ventures like these? What human qualities does it take to shape them over the years? This book, as its story unfolds, seeks to answer these two questions. This edition covers the sixty-four years of the Sir Dorabji Tata Trust (1932-96). The minutes of the Trust tell some of the inside story of the long debate and discussion, of the caution and daring, of the long anxious days and the moments of gratification born of tasks well accomplished. I have drawn on them freely along with other sources of information, personal and documentary. Whenever possible, I have tried to present the story as a story of people, sometimes of those who have benefited from Trust activities, at other times of those who have shaped, inspired, steered it. Some of the names are not known. A few, though important, have shunned the limelight, but their steady work over decades has taken the institutions the Trust established—and through them, one might say, the country—some bold steps forward. Inevitably, some names may have been missed out. Some may not have received their full due. Such omissions are unintentional.

The book was started in July 1981 and the first edition was completed in February 1982. I came from outside to study the Trust. The more I got involved in it the more fascinated I became. It opened for me the world of philanthropy in its widest sense. I saw it not so much as a story of Institutes and of grants made, but as a story of people and how their lives have been affected by the vision and magnanimity of the Founder coupled with the dedication and competence of those who administered it.

Some months after it was written, I was invited to join the

Trust, an invitation I accepted. In 1985 I was appointed its Director.

Since it was first published in 1984, interest in philanthropy has grown more so in the last years with the corporate sector bringing its considerable resources in the field. Some of these corporate houses are seeking imaginative avenues to serve the community. It was felt that this book, out of print for some years, needs to be brought out in an updated edition. A great deal has happened between 1982 and 1996. Some Institutes like the TISS have almost doubled in their faculties and have widened their scope of subjects. The Tata Memorial Hospital, also founded by the Trust is on the brink of a major expansion. On a 60-acre plot in New Mumbai, a project primarily for education and research in cancer is proceeding ahead. In 1991 J.R.D. Tata inaugurated the buildings of the National Institute of Advanced Studies, Bangalore, and in 1996, after his death, the Trust has supported the starting of the J.R.D. Tata Centre for Ecotechnology by the M.S. Swaminathan Research Foundation in Madras.

While I have left the main structure of the book undisturbed, there have been substantial additions in updating this story.

I owe thanks to four people: Prof. R.D. Choksi, who managed the Trust for 40 years and from whose wisdom I have benefited; Mr. D.K. Malegamvala, who had the conviction that I should write the book; Mr. A.K. Banerjee, who read the first draft and suggested the title 'The Heartbeat of a Trust'; and, above all, Mr. J.J. Bhabha, without whose vision, this book would not have seen the light of day.

In writing this book it has been my purpose to capture the width and the scope, the originality and the romance of this distinguished Foundation. I have tried to highlight the human endeavour that enabled the Trust to reach out into the sensitive spheres of national life.

R.M. LALA

Mumbai, September 12, 1997

Part I

IN TRUST FOR THE PEOPLE

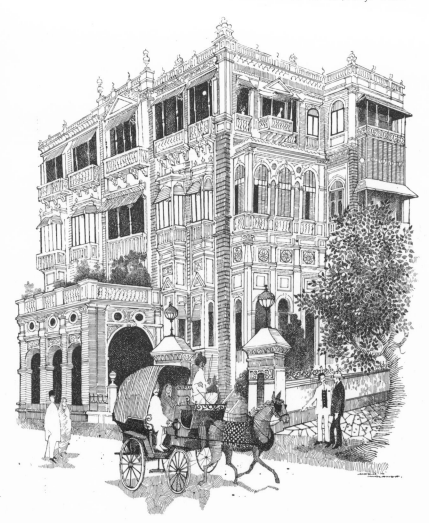

Esplanade House—The residence of Jamsetji and Sir Dorabji Tata

Chapter 1

The Genesis

It is not having that makes men great. A man may have the largest abundance of God's gifts — of money, of mental acquirements, of power, of heart possessions and qualities — yet if he only hoards what he has for himself, he is not great. Men are great only in the measure in which they use what they have to bless others. We are God's stewards, and the gifts that come to us are his, not ours, and are to be used for him as he would use them.

J.R. Miller in *'Green Pastures'*

Although charitable institutions existed in antiquity, the major foundations of today are the product of the wealth created by modern industry. The late 19th century witnessed the growth of the steel and oil industries in the United States which generated enormous financial resources. 'The good Lord,' said the first John Rockefeller, 'gave me my wealth.' In 1889 Andrew Carnegie wrote an essay on wealth in the *North American Review*. What exercised him was not the acquisition of dollars of which he had netted a fortune from steel-making, but the use of them. He devoted his later years to putting his resources to use for worthy purposes like the establishment of 2000 Public Libraries in the US and the UK. The problem of our age, he observed, is the proper administration of wealth. He believed that family pride and not the welfare of children inspired personal legacies to one's heirs. The thoughtful man must shortly say, 'I would as soon leave to my son a curse as [I would] the almighty dollar.' '[1]

---

1 Joseph Frazier Wall: *Andrew Carnegie*, Oxford University Press, New York, 1970.

In the late 19th century, when Carnegie and Rockefeller were exercised about the administration of their vast fortunes, Jamsetji Tata, who had also amassed wealth (albeit on a much smaller scale), was quite clear about its creative use. He wanted to utilise his wealth to bring about an industrial revolution in India. 'What advances a nation or community,' he said, 'is not to prop up its weakest and most helpless members as to lift up the best and most gifted, so as to make them of the greatest service to the country.' Jamsetji called this 'constructive philanthropy', and backed it up by starting in 1892 the J.N. Tata Endowment Fund and paid generous scholarships out of his own pocket—the first ones were Rs.10,000 of those days—about Rs.10 lakhs of today. Much later the Endowment was regularised with a corpus of Rs.25 lakhs for awarding scholarships to Indian students for higher studies abroad.

He established the Endowment Fund because he was eager that India should have her own doctors, lawyers, engineers and members of the Indian Civil Service, just then thrown open to Indians. Three decades later, one out of every five Indians in the ICS was a J.N. Tata Scholar.

In 1896, J.N. Tata conceived of establishing an institution of advanced scientific education and research, the like of which, according to his son Dorabji, even England did not have at that time. To finance this, he set aside 14 of his buildings and four landed properties. Unfortunately, Lord Curzon, the Viceroy, was lukewarm when the scheme was presented to him in 1899. But from 1896 onwards Jamsetji, in his Will and codicils to it, kept his benefaction untouched, in spite of discouragement from the British rulers. It was only in 1905, a year after Jamsetji's death, that Curzon gave the green light.

The Indian Institute of Science opened in Bangalore in 1911, and for the first four decades and more was the premier advanced institution for scientific work until the Tata Institute of Fundamental Research grew to share honours with it. In the last five years of his life, J.N. Tata also set in motion his two great schemes of setting up an integrated steel plant and of hydro-electric power generation. 'While many others worked at loosening the chains of slavery and hastening the march towards the dawn of freedom,' said Dr. Zakir Husain, 'Jamsetji dreamed of and worked for the life as it was to be fashioned after liberation. Most of the others worked for freedom from a bad life of servitude. Jamsetji worked for freedom for fashioning a better life of economic independence.'[2]

At the time of his death, Jamsetji's three great schemes still awaited fulfilment. Of his two sons, Dorabji and Ratan, it was Dorabji, with his drive and enthusiasm, and aided by the resolve of his cousin, R.D. Tata, who saw Jamsetji's projects through to the stage of accomplishment. It was Dorabji who explored Central India for iron ore, riding in bullock-carts, visiting places where they had to make even tea out of soda-water. He added many achievements of his own, and was knighted in 1910.

Sir Dorabji's finest hour came in 1924, when the ambitious expansion programme of Tata Steel ran into stormy weather. It was his audacity which had led the Company into undertaking a five-fold expansion programme in the post-war period. Spiralling prices, combined with transport and labour difficulties in the West, completely upset the price calculations. To aggravate this critical situation, Tata Steel's largest pig iron customer, Japan, was struck by an earthquake. Prices tumbled and, reeling under these blows, one timid Director suggested that the Government be asked to take over the Company. R.D. Tata, father of J.R.D. Tata, sprang to his feet, pounded the table and declared that that day would never come so long as he lived.

One day a telegram came from Jamshedpur to say that there was not enough money to pay the wages. Sir Dorabji and R.D. Tata set about raising funds. They went to the Imperial Bank where Sir Dorabji pledged his entire personal

---

2 Convocation Address to the Tata Institute of Social Sciences, 1962.

fortune worth about Rs. 1 crore (including his wife's personal jewellery) to obtain a loan—for a limited company. Tatas held about 11 per cent share in Tata Steel at the start and the proportion was probably much less by 1924.

It was touch and go. Sir Dorabji's willingness to sacrifice everything paid off. The first returns from expanded production came in and the Company got a breather and finally survived. Sir Dorabji had grit; he had confidence in the intrinsic soundness of the enterprise and took a calculated risk.

At Jamsetji's death, the Tata enterprises comprised three textile mills and the Taj Mahal Hotel, Bombay. Under Sir Dorabji Tata's stewardship were added an integrated steel plant—then the largest single unit in the British empire—three electric power companies, a large edible oil and soap company, two cement companies, one of India's leading insurance companies and an aviation unit pioneered by J.R.D. Tata. The airline was to blossom into Air-India, the country's national carrier. Meanwhile, Sir Dorabji had also seen through the establishment of the Indian Institute of Science, Bangalore, that was to spearhead scientific research in India for decades to come. Proud as he was of these achievements, he never failed to give due credit to his father's pioneering spirit. 'Kind fate,' he once noted, 'has ... prompted me to help in bringing to completion his (Jamsetji's) inestimable legacy of service to the country.'

Dorabji was born on August 27, 1859, when Jamsetji was 20 years old. After attending the Proprietory High School in Bombay, he was sent at the age of 16 to a private tutor in Kent. At 18, he entered the Gonville and Caius College at Cambridge. During the two years he was there, he distinguished himself at sports, winning colours at Caius for cricket, rugger and soccer. He also played tennis for his college, coxed his college boat, won a number of sprint events, and was a good horseman. A robust young man, he returned to Bombay in 1879, joined St. Xavier's College and obtained his B.A. in 1882.

Dorabji's love of sport was abiding. To him India owes

Gonville and Caius College, Cambridge

her first participation in the Olympic Games. In 1919, before India had set up an Olympic Committee, he selected and financed four athletes and two wrestlers for participation in the Antwerp Games in 1920. He secured for India a place in the 1924 Paris Olympics. He was chosen to be a member of the International Olympic Committee. In the 1928 Olympics at Amsterdam, India won the Gold Medal for hockey. Sir Dorabji had the country scoured for sports talent and arranged for the then Director of the YMCA to tour the country and bring home to the people of India the importance of the Olympic movement. He helped to found, amongst other institutions, the Willingdon Sports Club and the Parsi Gymkhana in Bombay, the High Schools Athletic Association, and the Bombay Presidency Olympic Games Association. As President of the Indian Olympic Council, he financed the Indian contingent to the Paris Olympiad of 1924.

What kind of a person was Sir Dorabji. At the time of writing this revised edition 64 years after his death, the only living person who knew him well was the nephew of his wife, Lady Meherbai Tata, Jamshed J. Bhabha. In 1995, on the occasion of inaugurating a statue of Sir Dorabji at Jamshedpur, Mr. Bhabha first related the significant contribution of Sir Dorabji and then gave interesting insights into the personality of Sir Dorabji. Relating from boyhood memories of Sir Dorabji, Mr. Bhabha said:

'In addition to being a "blue" for cricket at Cambridge, Dorabji was a life-long admirer of the renowned cricketer of those Victorian days, W.G. Grace, great as a batsman and also great in physical size. He was a boyhood hero of Dorabji who had collected in both Esplanade House and in his Poona house, "Gladhurst", a number of pictures and cartoons of W.G. Grace by the cartoonist, famous then, ZPY, and others.

'When the first M.C.C. team ever to come to India, visited Bombay under the captaincy of Gilligan, Dorabji gave a lunch in their honour in the spacious Moorish Room of Esplanade House, the home of the Founder who had planned every detail of it. The room had a huge oblong table capable of seating about 50 guests. Its unique feature was that food dishes could be served by waiters, not from behind and between the guests in the usual inconvenient fashion, but from a large central well in the middle of the oblong table. The dishes were brought by the serving staff into this central well direct from the kitchen through an underground tunnel. Jamsetji, surprisingly, did not use this innovative arrangement in his Taj Mahal Hotel to which also he gave so much of his creation.

'On week days, my elder brother Homi and I used to cross the road from the Cathedral School to have lunch and tea at Esplanade House. At the small lunch table in the Japanese Room decorated with beautiful Japanese and Chinese plates and porcelain which now embellish sections of the Prince of Wales Museum, Homi would be seated on the right of our aunt Meherbai, with me, just ten years old, next to him and therefore next to our formidable uncle Dorabji, our father, Jehangir, being seated on the opposite side of the table. While the four of us enjoyed a good three-course lunch, Dorabji who was by then badly diabetic, would be served an austere and measured plateful of boiled slices of vegetables such as brinjal, tomatoes and beans. It is no wonder that he would soon clean out the plate.

'One day a new Gujarati servant, instead of just removing the empty plate, asked him if he had finished. Dorabji turned to glare and said in Gujarati, "Can't you see I'm hungry and I still have to eat the plate?"

'He used to come with Meherbai Fui (and we children called him Dorabji Fua) for dinner once a week at our Pedder Road house when they would bring engaging toys for us children. As young children we were not allowed to join the dinner table and were sent off to have our meal separately while the elders were still having drinks. Important political figures of those days would be invited to dinner on such occasions such as the two great Muslim leaders of the "Kilafat" movement, Maulana Mohammed Ali (who was at Oxford with my father as one of the only nine Indians then at the

University who clubbed together to form what they called the "Nav-Ratan") and his usually tall big brother, Maulana Shaukat Ali. Mohammed Ali Jinnah was indirectly related to my mother through his marriage with Rati Petit.

'Diabetes had made Dorabji crotchety in his old age, but through most of his life, he was good-humoured, witty and full of comic stories and anecdotes. Only one of the many books of humour and wit that he had in his collection is available today, namely, "The Table In A Roar", illustrated by the then great cartoonist, W.H. Bateman.'

At the age of 38 Dorabji married 18-year-old Meherbai (fondly called 'Mehri'), daughter of H.J. Bhabha, Inspector-General of Education, Mysore State. Meherbai was a beautiful and an accomplished lady. She was fond of English literature and played the piano with a sensitive touch. Prior to her marriage, Mehri was in demand at every concert performance in Mysore. Jamsetji seems to have had a hand in the selection of Mehri as his daughter-in-law. He used to visit Mysore regularly from 1890 onwards as he foresaw the industrial potential of that State. It is on these visits that he came in close contact with the Bhabha family. It is recorded that in 1897, on Dorabji proposing to Mehri, Jamsetji wrote to Mehri expressing, in the warmest terms, his admiration for her. She shared with Dorabji a love of sport and especially of tennis at which she once won the triple crown in the Western India Tennis Tournament. Sir Stanley Reed, Editor of *The Times of India,* a close friend of the family, speaking about the completion by Sir Dorabji of his father's dreams called it:

> one of the economic romances of our rather materially-minded Bombay.... But this would never have been accomplished if Sir Dorabji had not seen his purpose with wide open eyes; if he had not had always at his side a wife who was as staunch in the pursuit of these filial and patriotic duties as himself. Lady Tata was one of the clearest brains it has ever been my lot to find in woman. No one could put her own case with more convincing logic.[3]

---

3 *Lady Tata: A Book of Remembrance,* privately published, Bombay, 1932. Foreword by Sir Stanley Reed. The book includes a 'Life Sketch' by K. Natarajan.

Lady Meherbai

In the first years of their marriage Meherbai moved in a small circle. Spirited and sensitive, she was deeply concerned about the condition of women. At the age of 38 she made a mark on the national scene by heading a deputation to the Viceroy to protest against the treatment accorded to indentured labour of Indian origin in the British colonies like the Fiji islands, winning the acclaim of Mrs. Sarojini Naidu for her presentation. In the years to follow she became one of the founders, first of the Bombay Presidency Women's Council and then of the National Council of Women. She was consulted on the Sarda Act designed to outlaw child marriage. She campaigned for higher education for women and against the purdah system and the practice of untouchability. In view of developments in the 1990s when a move is afoot for the Parliament of India to reserve one-third of its seats for women, it is significant that 70 years earlier Lady Meherbai's was one of the first — if not the first voice — for the entry for more women into the legislatures.

'Her great belief,' said Lady Dinshaw Mulla, 'is that the resurrection of India would only come by and through the advancement of our womanhood.' Lady Tata introduced India into the International Council of Women when many others felt that India should concentrate on her internal freedom struggle. In so doing she brought India into the women's international movement, as her husband brought India into the world Olympic movement.

A contemporary writing, in a London newspaper, recalls one moment of her life—her appearance at the International Council of Women in London:

> Besides ropes of wonderful pearls, which are so becoming to her creamy complexion, Lady Tata is the possessor of the largest privately owned diamond in the world.... Absolutely flawless, and weighing 245 carats, the Jubilee Diamond is oval in shape and faultless in lustre, brilliance and purity. It is set in a platinum claw and worn as a pendant on a thin platinum chain.[4]

---

4 Quoted in *Lady Tata: A Book of Remembrance*, op. cit. For further details on the Jubilee Diamond see Appendix J.

With inborn dignity, Lady Tata could move with royalty abroad and at the same time involve herself in earthy issues at home. On one occasion, when she heard that the women of Byculla in Bombay were unable to get vegetables because of riots, she organised a group of ladies and wanted the permission of the Police Commissioner to sell vegetables. Looking at the distinguished delegation, the then British Police Commissioner said that he would not mind their giving away the vegetables as charity, but it would not look 'graceful' for women like them to sell vegetables. At that point Lady Tata tapped the table and said firmly, 'We have come here to be useful, not graceful.'

Lady Tata was about 50 when she was struck by leukaemia. Within a year, on June 18, 1931, while she was at Ruthin, North Wales, she died.

Lady Meherbai and the Police Commissioner

Sir Dorabji and Lady Tata had no children. Like his father before him, Sir Dorabji believed that wealth must be put to constructive use, and less than a year after his wife died, on March 11, 1932, he put all his wealth, estimated at Rs. 1 crore, into a trust for use, 'without any distinction of place, nationality or creed', for the advancement of learning and research, the relief of distress, and other charitable purposes. This was the beginning of the Sir Dorabji Tata Trust. Soon after this, in April of the same year, as a memorial to his wife, he endowed the Lady Tata Memorial Trust with a corpus of Rs. 25 lakhs for research into leukaemia,[5] and a much smaller trust, partly from public donations, the Lady Meherbai D. Tata Education Trust, for the training of women in hygiene, health and social welfare. This was done in an era when, unlike today, no tax benefits accrued to the settlor of a charitable trust.

All his life Sir Dorabji was absorbed in his sizeable industrial enterprises. But way back in 1912, as the Institute at Bangalore was getting on its feet, he offered it a donation as large as his father's to establish a School of Research in Tropical Medicine. The then Director felt that the infant institute would find it difficult to manage so major a project and that it would divert the Institute from the purpose for which it had been established and the offer was declined. In 1920 Sir Dorabji donated £25,000 to the University of Cambridge for the equipment of a laboratory in the School of Engineering. He endowed a Chair of Sanskrit at the Bhandarkar Oriental Institute. During his lifetime he also gave to the Prince of Wales Museum, Bombay, his collection of paintings, statuary and other art objects, now on display there as the Sir Dorabji Tata Collection. His brother, Sir Ratan,

---

5　Four-fifths of the awards were for international scientists and researchers in this field and one-fifth for Indian scientists. In 1953, at a World Congress on Leukaemia, held by CIBA, in London, it was found that one out of every three delegates had at one time or another been a recipient of a grant from this Trust. For the year 1995-96 the Trust put at the disposal of its International Committee in London a sum of pounds 200,000 (Rs. 1 crore) from which researchers were given grants.

had earlier made a donation of his art collection, including Chinese jade, to the same museum.

In his later years, Sir Dorabji Tata, due to an aggravation of his chronic diabetes, seems to have become an irritable, lonely, suspicious man, accepting few as his friends. Those who knew him towards the end of his life speak of him as 'a holy terror' to younger people and caustic in his remarks to his colleagues. But this could never diminish the achievement of the earlier years and his signal final contribution—the establishment of a substantial trust into which he poured all his wealth, down to the last pearl-studded tie-pin.

Early in 1932, the idea of a radium institute was suggested to Sir Dorabji by the Governor of Bombay, Sir Frederick Sykes. He decided to start the necessary enquiries and, in the course of his impending visit to Europe he hoped to seek advice in London on the proposal.

On April 11, 1932, Sir Dorabji set sail for Europe expecting, among other things, to visit his wife's grave in England. It was on this journey that, on June 3, he died at Bad Kissingen, Germany. A few days later, almost on the anniversary of his wife's death, he was laid beside her at the Brookwood Cemetery. The mausoleum in which they both rest is designed on the model of that of Cyrus the Great of Persia. On the lintel above the door is the family crest and motto from the Zoroastrian scriptures:

Humata	Hukhta	Hvarshta
Good	Good	Good
thoughts	words	deeds

The words are flanked on either side by Persian rosettes. Also designed from an ancient Persian model, the sarcophagus is of green bronze and stands on a marble plinth. It bears on its two sides the names:

DORAB — MEHRI

In her own lifetime Lady Tata gave freely of herself for the causes she believed in. In the evening of his life her husband placed all he had in trust. At the time he constituted it in March 1932, he probably had no idea that the first two ventures that the Trust bearing his name was to undertake were to be linked with his wife. One was the Sir Dorabji Tata Graduate School of Social Work. His wife was a social worker and her last address to the Bombay Presidency Women's Council was on social service. The second project the Trust was to undertake was the establishment of the first major cancer hospital in the East. It was of cancer of the blood that she had died.

Sir Dorabji had thought of setting up a radium wing in a Bombay hospital. But something much bigger was ultimately to emerge in memory of his wife, an institution which was to give hope and a new lease of life to thousands from all over Asia and even Africa. It was the Tata Memorial Hospital, India's first and to date the leading Hospital for the treatment, teaching and research into cancer.

Chapter 2

The Trust in Action

Under his Trust Deed, Sir Dorabji bequeathed certain landed properties, shares and securities, trinkets, ornaments, jewellery, and Rs. 23 lakhs standing to his credit in Tata Sons, to the Trust.[1] The total estate was valued at Rs. 1 crore in 1932, equivalent to about Rs. 83.4 crores today.

The purposes of the Trust were:

Institution, maintenance and support of schools, educational institutions, hospitals;

Relief of distress caused by the elements of nature such as famine, pestilence, fire, tempest, flood, earthquake or any other calamity;

Advancement of learning in all its branches, especially research work in connection with medical and industrial problems;

Financially aiding the Indian Institute of Science, Bangalore, in instituting professorships or lecturerships or giving scholarships;

Awarding fellowships in any branch of science or assisting students to study abroad either by payment of lump sums or by payment of periodical sums; and

Giving aid to any other charitable institutions or objects endowed by the settlor in his lifetime, or by the grandfather, father or brother of the settlor.

The Trustees were empowered to sell Sir Dorabji's lands, shares, securities and jewellery. The jewellery and landed

---

1 This was done under an agreement between Sir Dorabji as the 'settlor' of the Trust of the one part and Lady Ratan Tata, Nowroji Saklatvala (who was to succeed Sir Dorabji as Chairman of Tata Sons), Sorab Saklatvala, J.R.D. Tata, Jivaji Gandhy (Tata's solicitor), N. M. Mazumdar and Sir Dorabji, as Trustees, of the other part.

properties were sold by them in 1937, when prices were fairly depressed—even the fabulous Jubilee Diamond fetching less than what Sir Dorabji is reputed to have paid for it in 1900.[2] The Rs. 23 lakhs Sir Dorabji had to his credit with Tata Sons, the Trustees were not permitted to withdraw during such time as the executors of the Wills of, or the Trustees of Sir Dorabji, Sir Ratan Tata and R.D. Tata held the majority of shares in the firm. In this way, through the Trust, he sought to ensure the integrity of the parent firm his father, he and R.D. Tata had founded in 1887.

As neither Sir Ratan nor Sir Dorabji had any children, their holdings could well have been fragmented and with them Tata Sons. The Trusts[3] Sir Dorabji and Sir Ratan set up gave to Tata Sons a cohesive and a continuing character over decades to follow.

It is one thing to establish a large trust; it is another to administer it effectively. Charitable trusts go back many centuries and both Indian custom and Roman law acknowledge their existence, but the major modern foundations originated only in the early years of this century. Though Jamsetji Tata demonstrated his vision and munificence in founding the J.N. Tata Endowment for the Higher Education of Indians in 1892 and providing for the founding of the Indian Institute of Science, Bangalore, his philanthropy did not establish a single, multipurpose foundation. That was left to his younger son, Sir Ratan, who died in 1918.

Under the terms of his Will, the Sir Ratan Tata Trust was established in 1919, one of the first major Indian foundations in the modern sense of the word. The Sir Dorabji Tata Trust, as has been already mentioned, was established in 1932. Both these Trusts broke out of customary constraints of

---

2 Appendix J.
3 Details of the Tata Trusts are in Appendix A.

community and religion, common features of most Indian trusts of those days. Both rank amongst the first largest Indian foundations of a national character, both were multipurpose institutions and both were seeking suitable avenues for their activities.

In 1932, Lady Ratan Tata invited F.S. Markham of the Museum Association, London, to advise the Sir Ratan Tata Trust on how best it should proceed in the attainment of the objectives of the donor. Sir Dorabji Tata Trust, which had just been set up also took this opportunity to seek Mr. Markham's views on its own proposed activities. Mr. Markham, on his return to England in July 1933, advised that the Sir Dorabji Tata Trust 'embark upon a definite three- or five-year policy, with the intention of securing the greatest possible advance in one or two main directions'.

Markham's advice only confirmed the thinking of the Trustees and of the late Sir Dorabji, whose primary objective was not to fritter away energies and resources in multifarious projects but to launch on the founding of institutions that individuals, even with foresight, were unable to do for lack of resources. The Trust was soon to establish two major institutions, one for social work and the other for the treatment of cancer. It was along the same lines that the Tata Institute of Fundamental Research and the National Centre for the Performing Arts were to come later. These institutions initiated by the Trust were to be nurtured by it over a formative period of many years.

During this period of nurturing which extended to between 20 and 25 years in the case of the Hospital and the Tata Institute of Social Sciences (TISS), the Trust was ultimately responsible for the financing. From the very start the Tata Institute of Fundamental Research (TIFR) was carried jointly with the co-operation of the Central and State Governments. Representatives of the Trust are on the Governing Council of the respective institutions in perpetuity. In 1954 the Tata Memorial Hospital was handed over to the nation and is now financed by the Atomic Energy

Commission. Since 1964, the University Grants Commission deemed the TISS as a University and has been the main financier.

The objectives of the Trust are wide-ranging and the years have brought increasing and varied responsibilities. Education, medical relief, disaster relief—each making its own demands in a country where 70 per cent of the people live below the poverty line. With the magnitude of the problems facing India, how does one set one's priorities? What are the criteria for decision-making, for deciding to assist one project and declining to assist another? How does a multipurpose service organisation like the Sir Dorabji Tata Trust operate in such circumstances?

The task that the Dorabji Tata Trust—or any major Indian multipurpose trust—faces is far more challenging and complicated than that confronted by multipurpose trusts in the West. In the West, the State assumes a major role as the guardian of the social interests of its people. A single day at the Sir Dorabji Tata Trust's office in Bombay may bring a frantic telegram from the Relief Commissioner, Orissa, where floods have devastated vast areas; an appeal from the principal of a School for Deaf Children; a polite request from a Vedic Research Institute for a sustained grant for preparing an Avesta etymological dictionary; and a plea from a widow with cancer, whose husband has recently died. It is not uncommon for even an executive, suddenly confronted with a bill of Rs. 150,000 for open-heart surgery, to apply for a grant. The Trust gives no loans.

Most individual applications are requests for medical or educational grants or to meet a distress situation. Those who apply for medical grants get a standard form to fill in details about their medical condition, their other sources of finance and relevant certificates to assist the Trust in taking a decision. The policy of the Trust is to help individuals become self-supporting and not to provide doles. Recurring grants are not advisable. With the proliferation of conferences the world over, travel grants just to read papers or to attend Congresses are not encouraged. Those who bring back their expertise to India may be encouraged more readily.

There are also appeals from institutions, universities, colleges, schools and hospitals. Then there are institutes interested in subjects ranging from mountaineering to yoga, and those that look after the physically or mentally handicapped. A pioneer spastic society may want a grant to train teachers and a society for the mentally handicapped may request that the salary of an instructor be underwritten for a couple of years. The Trust receives some 2,000 such applications from institutions each year, each of which is to be attended. Up to half of these are sanctioned.

Some heads of institutions call personally, others may be requested to call. Background and supporting papers have to be collated for each appeal and a summary made on each institute. Utilisation of previous grants to them, if any, and, when possible, their general performance are assessed. Occasional visits are undertaken for an on-the-spot study. These results are presented for Group Discussion to the senior officers of the Trust. The cases of some institutions are settled very quickly, on the basis of the facts presented, but on others there may be substantial and animated discussion, with different members of the Group expressing their views quite freely. At times they may differ and debate till a consensus is reached or the Director gives the final ruling. The Group then forwards its recommendations to the Trustees.

An important consideration in its assessment of applications from institutions, apart from the merit of the activities with which they are concerned, is the dedication of those who run them. Also, even if the Trust is favourably inclined in a particular case, it has to balance its contributions among the various demands that press upon it, and it may not be able to help or to help to the extent it would have liked.

If the grant recommended falls below a certain limit, the Managing Trustee is empowered to sanction it; if it exceeds the limit, a précis is circulated among all the Trustees for their assent. When major national calamities strike or a scheme of vital national importance is involved, the Chairman or one of the Trustees might himself take the initiative even in the absence of an application. The Board of Trustees[4] meets twice a year to review the working of the Trust and annually approves its budget.

Individuals and institutions are often happy to receive even a modest contribution as a recognition from the Dorabji Tata Trust, which serves as a door-opener to contributions from elsewhere.

The Trust has some ongoing schemes like 36 scholarships in the Indian Institute of Science, Bangalore. Further, it supports about 60 Sir Dorabji Tata Merit Scholars, the cream of the top nine Bombay colleges, who are selected while in Standard XII on the basis of their academic and extra-curricular excellence. If their performance remains good, they continue as Tata Scholars till they get their first degree (that is, for up to 6 years in the case of those studying medicine or engineering). Some are under the misapprehension that just because they get high distinction they are eligible for a scholarship. On compassionate or special grounds a scholarship is considered at University, vocational, engineering and medicine. School scholarships are not normally considered.

The Trust has been fortunate in its Chairmen. After the first meeting at which Sir Dorabji presided, for the following six years Sir Nowroji Saklatvala, the Head of Tata Sons, was its Chairman. Thanks largely to him, the cancer hospital project took off in the 1930s, despite numerous difficulties, and doubts and hesitation in some quarters. It was he who encouraged Clifford Manshardt to start the Sir Dorabji Tata Graduate School of Social Work.

Sir Nowroji was succeeded as Trust Chairman in 1938 by

---

4 See Appendix B for composition of the Trust.

his cousin, Sir Sorab Saklatvala, during whose term the Tata Institute of Fundamental Research was established. Sir Sorab did much to ease matters and free Dr. Homi Bhabha from routine administration so that he could engage more fully in his scientific pursuits. Former Union Finance Minister, Dr. John Matthai as Chairman took the Trust into rural welfare work in the early fifties when such work was still a novelty. Sir Homi Mody had a good spell as Chairman after John Matthai, to be succeeded in 1969 by J.R.D. Tata. While Mr. Tata had shed all his company chairmanships, his position as Chairman of the Trust he retained till the end of his life in 1993. He was succeeded as Chairman by Mr. Ratan N. Tata. Mr. J.J. Bhabha has been Managing Trustee since 1980 and later became Vice-Chairman.

A Trust official has to take decisions on requests that he or she processes every day. Recommendations are put up whether to help or to regret, or to discuss. Applicants may be called for an interview. Applications that come to the officer's desk range from requests, for example, for kidney transplants to scholarships.

The Trust may occasionally go out of its way to support a deserving case. For example, a 48-year-old lady had had five hip operations. She had a job as a physiotherapist at a leprosy hospital. Commuting in the Bombay buses was difficult for her. She requested a contribution towards a three-wheeler converted for her convenience. The Trust felt the case had all the elements that needed support. The Trust not only made sure the balance was found but got the vehicle released on a priority basis.

Even when no application is made an unsolicited grant from the Trust is not to be ruled out. For example, in the wake of communal riots in 1992-93 when some firemen were injured on duty, the Trust read in the papers about a welfare fund for firemen and their families, and took the trouble to track down the fund and contributed.

The first essential of a good Trust official is that he or she should keep the heart sensitive to human suffering. The next essential is not to allow oneself to become captive to one's sensitivity or viewpoint. The third essential is to have a wider perspective rather than a pine-headed approach that 'I am right'. The fourth is to be open to fresh truths and learning based on observations and experience and not just on reading reports or hearsay.

Work in the Trust office is with people. Each letter, each file, represents a person, his hopes, his dreams. At times a Trust decision may substantially determine a person's future. One Trust official keeps in mind the words of Count Leo Tolstoy:

> Men think that there are circumstances when they can treat their fellow being without love, but no such circumstances exist. Inanimate objects may be dealt with without love but human beings cannot be treated without love.... If you feel no love for men— leave them alone. Occupy yourself with things, with your own self, with anything you please, but not with men.

The performance of a Trust depends not so much by the size of the funds it disburses, but by the calibre of its Trustees and the staff who work in it. Its officials often determine the quality of its giving.

Sir Dorabji did not live to see the Trust he initiated blossom, but he had, before his death, extended his support to the good work being done in Bombay by a young American missionary, Dr. Clifford Manshardt. Soon after Sir Dorabji's death Dr. Manshardt was called upon by the Trust to study and make recommendations concerning the policy it should adopt. He was later invited to serve as adviser to the Trust and as its first Director from 1936-41.

To Dr. Manshardt goes much of the credit for giving a constructive, nation-building thrust to the work of the Trust. He was also the architect of its first major project to which the next chapter of this book is devoted.

Dr. Manshardt was succeeded as Director in 1941 by Professor Rustum D. Choksi who was later to become the Managing Trustee (1950-80). So intimate was Professor

Choksi's involvement with the affairs of the Trust for some forty years that there is no better way of conveying a picture of the Trust today than to give some account of the man and his personal contribution to its development.

When he came to the Sir Dorabji Tata Trust, Professor Rustum D. Choksi was Professor of English and Latin at

R to L: Pandit Jawaharlal Nehru at the opening of the new buildings of the Tata Institute of Fundamental Research with Dr. Homi Bhabha, Mr. J.R.D. Tata and Professor Rustum Choksi

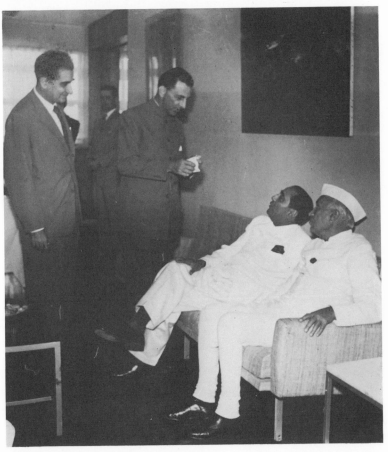

Wilson College, Bombay, a man full of energy and ideas. J.R.D. Tata encouraged him to continue his teaching so that he could have a live touch with the younger generation.

Among the galaxy whom he taught have been vice-chancellors, scholars and industrialists. V.K.R.V. Rao, eminent economist and former Union Minister for Education, who was his student, recalls that Professor Choksi was not much older than his students when Dr. Rao studied under him. V.K.R.V. Rao writes: 'Professor Choksi was always dressed in a white khadi suit with a khadi tie having an unusually large knot, and his clothes had an appearance of studied casualness that both thrilled and amused us. He had a most melodious voice and seemed to combine the Byronic handsomeness without the Byronic gloom and ... the wild but idealistic features of Shelley. He was easily our hero and I for one was greatly influenced by his charm, easy accessibility and friendly disposition that put me at ease, and succeeded in bringing out the best in my nature.'

Dr. (Miss) Usha Mehta, Professor of Politics, University of Bombay, and a well-known Gandhian, recalls the Professor's recitation of Shelley, Wordsworth and Keats in his ringing voice. She remembers him quoting from Milton's *Paradise Lost:* 'who overcomes by force hath overcome but half his foe.'

'These words', she said, 'not only reverberated in our ears for a long time but also made us understand the value of liberty as also of Gandhiji's message of conquering hatred by love and brute force by soul-force.'

A man of disciplined habits and precise memory, his khaddar clad upright figure has been familiar to Tata employees for decades. Self-effacing yet decisive, erudite and with considerable natural charm, he saw through to completion numerous Trust projects and, over the years, was instrumental in recommending grants totalling crores of rupees for worthy causes. Subordinating his own career as an academic of outstanding calibre, he devoted himself to making possible the realisation of the dreams and aspirations of others, like the late Dr. Homi Bhabha, alongside whom he faithfully stood for the first twenty years of the Tata Institute of Fundamental Research (TIFR).

Professor Choksi similarly gave to the other institutes the Trust was associated with—like the Tata Institute of Social Sciences, the Tata Memorial Hospital, and the Indian Institute of Science, Bangalore—an element of continuity over decades, based on an understanding of their needs. This understanding he also extended to his decision-making processes. Sometimes, when undecided, he would ponder and add, 'on compassionate grounds, let us give it.'

For Professor Choksi, a trust was 'a welfare institution and not a lending institution' and this determined his approach to appeals and projects. He impressed upon his juniors that Trust work was a 'service' and had a respectful approach to all those who came to it for funds. 'Sometimes we may have made mistakes but our intentions have been good,' he said. A man with wide interests, he considered each proposal or project with critical appreciation as he would look at an English author when giving a lecture. He looked upon the grantees of the Trust as its partners in social welfare. Coupled with his wide sympathies was an understanding of human frailties, which combination generated a compassionate approach to the pleas he received. But his compassion was free of sentimentality and his approach to proposals always a practical one. His decisions were based on searching enquiries.

In discussion, Professor Choksi was patiently persuasive and unfailingly courteous and considerate. As S. S. Prabhu, a former Registrar of the Indian Institute of Science, Bangalore, said of Professor Choksi: 'He is a good listener and conducts discussions with an open mind.' As Chairman of the Institute's Governing Council, Professor Choksi created an atmosphere of freedom in which viewpoints could be freely expressed. On the rare occasions when discussions tended to become acrimonious, the Professor would drop in a gentle word or a soothing phrase, and harmony would return.

It is one thing to start an institute, it is another and much more difficult task to nourish it. In this task of nourishing and helping the growth of the autonomous institutes sponsored by the Trust, Professor Choksi played a distinguished part. As J.R.D. Tata said, it was he 'who set the tone and gave the leadership' to the Trust. He took an active interest in Trust affairs till he died in 1986 at the age of 84.

The nature of this leadership, its quality and foresight, were well illustrated in the following extract from a note by Professor Choksi on the proposal that led to the setting up of the Tata Institute of Fundamental Research:

> What distinguishes a Trust is not its ability to give or the extent or range of its giving but the character of its giving. It is important for a Trust to maintain its 'pioneering' character and this can only be done adequately where from time to time a Trust initiates and fosters new institutions and new types of service to society. For a great Trust the large project, carefully designed and executed, must always be a major objective. Even in the routine giving of grants and donations the Trust must constantly bear in mind the 'pioneering' factor.

This, it may well be said, expresses the philosophy of the Sir Dorabji Tata Trust, in the shaping of which Professor R. D. Choksi played a major role.

Jamshed Bhabha, who has succeeded Professor Choksi as Managing Trustee, and who has been associated with him for four decades, remarks that 'Professor Choksi exercised a deep and beneficent influence in the organisation and its relations with the staff. To his colleagues in the Trusts and on the Board of the parent firm of Tata Sons, he was a source of confidence and strength.' Mr. Bhabha often recalls the Professor's learning, wisdom and maturity of judgement and his innate humanity.

The first big venture of the Trust was to start in a rather unusual locality.

Part II

TATA INSTITUTE

OF

SOCIAL SCIENCES

Chapter 3

A Long-Distance Championship

You are the first of a new line of public servants. You seek fullness of life for the people of India, an enterprise in which you have the right to ask all men of good will to join you. The fulfilment of this enterprise will not come as a fully developed Utopia; it must be built up family by family, neighbourhood by neighbourhood, community by community, village by village, city by city, state by state — it is not a hundred yard dash; it is a long-distance championship.

Visiting Professor Dr. Arthur E. Holt
speaking to the first group of
graduates passing out

Six roads meet at Nagpada, the geographical centre of Bombay. Standing tall at the crossroads, 50 years ago, was the statue of a Parsi philanthropist perched on a pillared pedestal. The gentleman and the site were simply called *Khada Parsi*, Standing Parsi, as hardly anyone could remember his name—or see his face! If the gentleman could have surveyed the neighbourhood, he would have found, crowded around him, a most colourful community of people. To the south-east lay Mohammedali Road, one of the largest Muslim concentrations in the city; elsewhere were colonies of Hindus, and somewhere, in between, were Iraqi Jews. Nagpada was, however, as insanitary as it was intriguing. It had the highest death rate in Bombay. In these unwelcoming and needy surroundings, the American Marathi Mission decided to establish the Nagpada Neighbourhood House in 1927.

The activities of the House were to be recreational—games, boxing, wrestling, supervised play; educational—music, night school, adult education, drama; medical—a dispensary; and religious—emphasising not creed but 'stimulating all to a higher way of living.'

Diwan Bahadur Harilal Desai, Minister for Education for the Bombay Government, was invited to open the House. After some hesitation the Minister agreed to come and gave it his whole-hearted support. The principal address of the evening was given by the editor of the *Indian Social Reformer,* K. Natarajan.

In the preparation for the formal opening day and to ensure that all communities would participate in its activities jointly, paradoxically enough, through each day of the preceding week, a cinema show was held for each community separately. As the cinema was somewhat of a novelty in the 1920s, each evening a film was announced to ensure a good attendance. A contemporary describes what happened on one of the evenings:

> On Tuesday evening we especially invited our Mohammedan neighbours. The meeting was set for nine o'clock, but by 6.30 the compound was full of children waiting for the doors to open. We had to refuse admission to many, for even the most optimistic of us was surprised at the interest of our Mohammedan friends.... I explained our purpose in English, and a young teacher translated it into Urdu. Then we had a cinema. Our electrical connections were not perfect but the enthusiasm of the crowd did not waver. Everything that could possibly be cheered was cheered to the echo. The crowd felt at home. It shouted, smacked, spat red betel-nut juice upon the floor, and enjoyed itself to the full. It was with great difficulty that we were able to close. The Jewish and Hindu nights followed.

On the opening day there was great excitement. The promise of another film broke the ice, among the communities and all attended in large numbers as just a group of happy people. The Pathé Company agreed to lend an old hand-powered cinema projector and a few current comedies, including one with Harold Lloyd. The only man in the neighbourhood who could run the machine took his

Nagpada, 1930s

responsibilities so seriously that he felt the need of fortifying himself with country liquor. The film was as erratic as the operator. At times it was fast and clear; at times it was slow and practically invisible, and all the time it was flickery. But the people loved it. They laughed, shouted, clapped and stomped, giving full vent to their enjoyment. 'They may not have comprehended or agreed with talk about our brotherhood,' noted the Director, 'but they were certainly one in their appreciation of comedy.'

The formalities over, the Neighbourhood House settled down to its difficult task of social leavening. At the heart of this operation was the young athletic American, Clifford Manshardt, the Director, to whom a brief reference was made in the previous chapter. Dr. Manshardt was possessed of abounding energy. He was an efficient administrator and a shrewd judge of men and their motivation. He knew how to win people's interest in what he was trying to do for them, to involve them actively in the effort, so that they were no longer passive recipients of benefits. No task was too menial or too unimportant for him and, when necessary, he would not hesitate to roll up his sleeves and sweep the streets of the neighbourhood. He had a fine sense of humour. Over the years he gained considerable public recognition in Bombay and served on 30 social service committees, but· whenever the children of Nagpada saw him they would still call out *'Shinema-walla' 'Shinema-walla!'*

With his Indian assistant, Mr. Patet, he visited hundreds of families in the neighbourhood. By inviting them as families to the Neighbourhood House, he made sure that even orthodox ladies in *burqas* turned up every Tuesday to be taught homecraft. The ladies also felt free enough to shed their *burqas* and play games like table tennis and badminton. It was the highlight of their week. The Neighbourhood House was the only place their orthodox husbands allowed them to visit.

The Neighbourhood House became a hive of activity. Of the total population of Bombay, which was then just over a million, Manshardt could report at the year end that 170,000 people had used the facilities of the Neighbourhood House at 75 public gatherings. Medical treatment had been given to over 6,000 patients, 275 students were enrolled in the night classes. Children in Nagpada who previously had no facilities for recreation now had a place where they and teenagers were provided with facilities for games and other pastimes.

When Manshardt started his work, there were hardly any professional social workers in India. He therefore decided to hold six-week courses of study to train bright young people in social work. The topics covered were The Changing Family, Juvenile Delinquency, Crime and Criminology, Public Health, Mental Hygiene, Communalism, and Public Opinion. The students were given hostel accommodation for Re. 1/-, with an additional Rs. 20/- covering food for the entire period. 'Students,' said the Prospectus, 'must bring their own bedding and dishes (not cooking utensils).' The courses were brief, but a beginning had been made.

One of those who encouraged and assisted Dr. Manshardt in those early years was Sir Dorabji Tata. In 1932, when on leave in the US, Manshardt heard that Sir Dorabji, just before his death, had set up a large Trust for the encouragement of education and research in the medical, scientific and industrial fields and for the relief of distress. Manshardt was interested in social research and, as Sir Dorabji had contributed earlier to his ventures, he decided to ask the Trustees to support his projects. The Trustees were unable to offer any immediate assistance since the policy of the Trust had not yet been determined. Instead the Trustees asked Manshardt if he would study the general Trust situation and make recommendations on the policy the Dorabji Tata Trust should adopt. The assignment was accepted and Manshardt was able to outline certain general principles for the conduct of the Trust for the consideration of the Trustees.

It was during this period that Manshardt became acquainted with Sir Nowroji Saklatvala, KBE, Chairman of Tata Sons Limited, and of the Dorabji Tata Trust. Their acquaintance soon ripened into friendship. Sir Nowroji invited

Manshardt to scrutinise the various applications received, and report to the Trustees on their merit. The Marathi Mission granted Manshardt permission to undertake this work while continuing as Director of the Nagpada Neighbourhood House.

The policy of the Trust was emerging. Its chief interest would be in encouraging nation-building activities and projects which promised to contribute to national welfare. The thrust would be to take up projects which were beyond the means of an individual or a small organisation. At the same time the Trust continued to assist generously for relief work in the case of national calamities such as the Quetta and Bihar earthquakes of 1934. Its helping hand reached out even across our frontiers to assist victims of national calamities in China, Turkey and Greece.

In keeping with the policy that it had adopted, the Trust was looking for projects of dimensions worthy of the objectives and the munificence of its founder. The Trustees requested Manshardt to study the situation further, and to present a list of projects which he felt to be worthy of the Trust's support. He listed eighteen schemes which he felt to be of genuine importance to the national welfare. This list was discussed, and eventually three projects were short-listed, a teachers' training college for women, a post-graduate school of social work, and a radium institute for the treatment of cancer.

There was, in the 1930s, a definite shortage of trained women teachers in the Bombay Presidency, and there were few subjects of greater importance to the future welfare of India than the education of girls and women. Sir Dorabji and Lady Tata's spacious estate in Poona (Ruby Hall), the Trustees felt, would lend itself very well to a teachers' training college for women. The Trust was willing to deed the estate to the government for this purpose, and Manshardt went over to Poona to discuss the offer with the Director of Public Instruction. The Director turned out to be a rather sour and harassed Englishman nearing retiring age who seemed to Manshardt unwilling to face the physical effort involved in starting something new. The Director made very short work of the proposal, saying that he did not require any advice on the educational needs of the Presidency from 'a professional American philanthropist'. The Trust's major projects were thus reduced to two: a post-graduate school of social work and a radium institute.

The school of social work was naturally the scheme nearest to Manshardt's heart. In discussing it with Sir Nowroji Saklatvala, Manshardt noted that, in starting such a school, Tatas may well be giving birth 'to a troublesome child', for the opinions of a school of social work might at times be widely at variance with the opinions of its capitalistic parents. Sir Nowroji's reply was characteristic of him. 'Tatas,' he said, 'have had plenty of criticism in the past and will have plenty in the future. We are big enough to take it and, I hope, profit from it.'

There was, of course, no real conflict between the policies of the Trustees as industrialists handling a huge labour force and as persons managing the affairs of a trust. The Tata tradition of labour welfare went back to the 1880s when Jamsetji introduced hitherto unheard of welfare facilities in his Empress Mills at Nagpur. Under Sir Dorabji's Chairmanship, The Tata Iron and Steel Company, Jamshedpur, worked an 8-hour day from the very outset, when it had yet to be legally enforced even in England.[1] In 1912, Sir Ratan Tata initiated an annual grant to the London School of Economics for research into the causes of poverty and the means of its alleviation.[2] This ultimately led to the formation of what is now the LSE's Department of Social Sciences.

When the School was finally organised, the Trustees of the Sir Dorabji Tata Trust became the Trustees also of the Sir

---

1 For more particulars see Appendix A of the present writer's *The Creation of Wealth*, India Book House, Bombay, 1981 and 1992.

2 Listed in the library of the LSE are publications of the Ratan Tata Foundation and among them are some of the early social surveys undertaken on subjects like 'Casual Labour in the Docks' and 'Feeding of School Children'.

Dorabji Tata Graduate School of Social Work, and, says Manshardt, 'followed its affairs with the same intelligent interest that they followed their business enterprises.'

Manshardt was appointed Director of the School and Dr. J.M. Kumarappa, an experienced Indian educator with American post-graduate training, was his collaborator. Other initial members of the staff were Dr. T. Altmann, a well-qualified German Jew refugee, trained at the University of Munich, Dr. Behram Mehta, a Chancellor's Medallist of the Bombay University, and Dr. Arthur E. Holt, a Visiting Professor of Social Ethics from the University of Chicago.

The Bombay Sentinel

June 22, 1936

Important Landmark In Indian Educational History

Tata Institute Will Raise Social Uplift Work To Dignity Of Learned Profession

Speaking at the opening session of the Sir Dorabji Tata Graduate School of Social Work, Bombay this afternoon Dr. Clifford Manshardt, the Director of the School said:—

This informal opening session of the Sir Dorabji Tata Graduate School of Social Work may well be an important landmark in the educational history of India. India has always had social work. Men have always helped their neighbours in time of trouble. India has had and has to-day a long list of noteworthy social w~ There have been in of the count~ for the t' for '

lopment of public agencies supported by the public funds. Such departments of Government need competent administrators as well as able men and women who can do the rank and file work, especially that of individualizing and humanizing social treatment.

I turn now to a brief consideration of practical or field work. Just as the medical student gages in clinical work pital, so the sor takes field w

Because of the groundwork laid by Manshardt through the Neighbourhood House classes, it was possible to open the School within a few months of approval of the project by the Trust.

The budget Manshardt submitted was a modest one— Rs. 37,500/- for the first year.[3] His plan was not to spend on buildings at the start but to use the existing facilities of the Neighbourhood House. He himself moved out of his apartment on the top floor to make room for a library. He wisely decided to take only 20 students once in two years so as to ensure that each one got adequate guidance and instruction. He was also keen not to turn out more graduates than could initially be employed on a professional basis. The Trustees were, however, surprised by the response to the first advertisement of the Institute. Four hundred graduates applied for admission.

At the opening session of the School on June 22, 1936, Manshardt raised with his students the question: 'And if you say to yourselves, "What can twenty students do in the face of India's problem?" I would remind you that you twenty are but the beginning. Year by year, your number will increase and the time will come when trained social workers will be at work in every important centre in India.' Manshardt's dream has come true. Today there are over 66 schools of social work. The spirit of the training imparted is evidenced by what Manshardt told his students and at each convocation of the TISS about 120 students received their diplomas.

Manshardt said :

> It is our belief that this School is a part of life, and that its students should be trained to make independent judgements, to examine questions from all angles, and to build a life philosophy, which is their own, and not a pale imitation of those who have gone before.

> This School is not a coaching college. It is not preparing you to pass a certain examination. It is endeavouring to help you to a philosophy of life .... We supplement classroom work with practical

---

3 Rs. 9,37,000 of 1995

field work—for we do not want our students ever to forget that their fundamental problem as social workers is not books but people.

Since social work deals in some measure with deviations from normal behaviour, an effort was made to train the students in the tackling of human problems. The course included training in family and child psychology, historical background to social work, India's social problems, rural-urban interaction, the industrial worker, industrial legislation, and the state and social work. Another group of courses dealt with the practice of social work—casework, group work, a labour officer's work and administration of social work. Everyone took all the subjects. There was no specialisation.

It was decided from the beginning that the School would not be attached to any existing university so that it remained free to develop its own curriculum. It, therefore, had no inducement to offer in the shape of a degree, so precious to the Indian student. It simply granted its own diploma to successful candidates on completion of the two-year course. As many graduates who initially applied had no background in social sciences, the Institute offered courses to make up for this deficiency.

The School came into existence when the world was emerging from the economic depression of the early thirties and just before the first Congress Government assumed office in the then Bombay Presidency in 1937. From the day the School started there was hardly a day when the mail did not bring requests for some information concerning social problems. The strength of the School was that it was rooted in ten years of practical experience at the Neighbourhood House, set in the midst of the harsh realities of Nagpada. It was not an Institute conceived in the West and planted in India. 'Here centres a whole constellation of voluntary public services which would be notable anywhere in the world,' said an American Visiting Professor and continued, 'here is something more authoritative than theory,'—the influence of people who have lived and worked in the midst of the reality of problems. Speaking to the first group of graduating students, Visiting Professor Dr. Arthur E. Holt said:

> You are the first of a new line of public servants. You seek fullness of life for the people of India, an enterprise in which you have the right to ask all men of goodwill to join you. The fulfilment of this enterprise will not come as a fully developed Utopia; it must be built up family by family, neighbourhood by neighbourhood, community by community, village by village, city by city, state by state—it is not a hundred yard dash; it is a long-distance championship.

As the School of Social Work was dedicated to national service, Manshardt made every effort to introduce his students to prominent national leaders. The Premier of Bombay in the first Congress Ministry, B.G. Kher, presided at the first convocation (1938), where Dr. Radhakamal Mukherjee delivered the address. Dr. B.R. Ambedkar and Pandit Jawaharlal Nehru were also invited to address the faculty and students. Both spoke on untouchability, though on different occasions. The second convocation, 1940, was addressed by Mrs. Sarojini Naidu; the third, 1942, by Sir Rustom Masani; and the fourth, 1944, by Dr. S. Radhakrishnan.

The objective of the TISS was laid out with clarity by its founder-Director Clifford Manshardt at the opening session of the Sir Dorabji Tata Graduate School of Social Work as it was then called. On 22nd June 1936 Dr. Manshardt said: 'A school of social work is not a graduate school of Economics or Sociology. While Sociology seeks to understand social phenomena, social work seeks to manipulate, change and control the materials with which it deals. Sociology seeks to understand the laws of human association, while social work seeks to apply these laws. The research activities of the School of Social Work are, therefore, eminently practical, dealing with the everyday problems of social life. But, though practical, the research for which this School stands is both scholarly and accurate. We want to know how to discover facts and how to interpret them to the best advantage they are found.'[4]

Clifford Manshardt had been a young soldier in France during World War I. He saw the futility of fighting as a means of solving human problems and pledged himself to work for the alleviation of conflict between races, nations and classes. 'During the years that followed,' he recalled, 'I have had many reasons to lose heart, but I have not abandoned my faith in humanity. Mankind may err. Large sections of the population may be misguided. But mankind is still the only resource upon which we can depend for social regeneration.'

Clifford Manshardt came to India in October 1925 and lived and worked here till June 1941. During his stay, he was in the mainstream of Indian life, as his book, *Pioneering on Social Frontiers in India,*[5] so vividly recounts. His invitations to nationalist leaders to address convocations and other gatherings at the Sir Dorabji Tata Graduate School of Social Work indicate that Manshardt did not attempt to disguise his sympathy for the Indian nationalist movement. In 1934, he permitted the use of the Nagpada Neighbourhood House by the Nationalist Christian Party, one of whose meetings was addressed by Khan Abdul Ghaffar Khan. For his thundering oration, Abdul Ghaffar Khan was awarded a two-year prison sentence; and Manshardt was placed under police surveillance.

When the War broke out in 1939, Manshardt was summoned by the Deputy Commissioner of Police, CID, and warned not to persist in his 'political indiscretions'—of which a huge dossier lay on the police officer's desk. Considering that the Dorabji Tata Trust was a strictly non-political body, it is to the credit of the Trustees that they did not ever

---

4 Extract form an address entitled "Education for Social Work" delivered at the opening session of the Sir Dorabji Tata Graduate School of Social Work, Bombay, June 22, 1936.
5 Lalvani Bros., Bombay, 1967.

suggest that Manshardt be disassociated from the Trust or that he disassociate himself from his nationalist connections.

Before he left India for reasons of family health in 1941, Dr. Manshardt recommended to the Trust that he be succeeded as Director of the Tata School of Social Work by his colleague and collaborator, Dr. J.M. Kumarappa, and as Director of the Trust by Professor Rustum D. Choksi. Both recommendations were readily accepted.

Chapter 4

Small Institution with Big Men

I have had many reasons to lose heart, but I have not abandoned my faith in humanity. Mankind may err. Large sections of the population may be misguided. But mankind is still the only resource upon which we can depend for social regeneration.

Dr. Clifford Manshardt
First Director of the
Tata Institute of Social Sciences
(1936-1941)

In the 19th century India witnessed not only the rise of individuals of conviction who cared for social reform, like Raja Ram Mohun Roy, but also the birth of movements of great vitality, like the Brahmo Samaj, the Arya Samaj and the Ramakrishna Mission. Though all of these had a religious basis, they were deeply interested in social reform.

While there were stirrings in India for social reform, it was the West that produced the first professionally trained social workers. 'Social Science, as distinguished from social reform, is a new feature of Indian life, which we owe chiefly to the example of Christian missions.'[1] When the Sir Dorabji Tata Graduate School of Social Work started, the impulse for social service existed but its techniques had not been developed or taught.

Dr. J. M. Kumarappa, who succeeded Clifford Manshardt as Director at the School of Social Work, was very different from the American activist. He was primarily a scholar with

---

1 Natarajan: *A Century of Social Reform in India,* Bombay, Asia Publishing House, Bombay, 1959.

an M.A. from Harvard and an M.A. and Ph.D. from Columbia. He studied social problems in depth. He wrote many books, including *Our Beggar Problem*. Pupils recall him as 'a friendly soft-spoken man' who came to the Institute dressed in a well-pressed suit and felt hat. He had a chauffeur-driven Pontiac car, large and dignified, in keeping with his personality.

Kumarappa's home was next door to the Neighbourhood House and often he used to work in his office till ten at night. In those early and pioneering days, the man who headed the Institute was also its chief public relations officer. It was to Kumarappa's credit that he continued Manshardt's traditions of getting the leading figures of the nation involved with the Institute. A member of the Rajya Sabha, he was much respected in Delhi.

To complement Kumarappa's style was Dr. Behram Mehta who, true to the Manshardt tradition, was ever ready for action in the field. An unconventional teacher, he used to argue with his students in the classroom. He would occasionally flay even the authorities of the School. He was not unlike Elam of Ernest Raymond's *Through Literature to Life*. Like Elam he was critical of those above him and he inspired the younger generation—in Mehta's case with a tremendous urge for social work. An entire generation of students, including Dr. Gore, later Director of the Tata Institute, and Professor Kaikobad (who also worked with the UN for 5 years) recall Dr. Mehta with gratitude. 'We were a class of fifteen,' recalls Dr. Gore, 'and some of the students were very poor. Dr. Mehta was very good to the poor boys and even found them part-time work.' Mehta would go camping with his students and no distance separated him from them. He refused to give his students ready-made solutions. 'Seek answers to your problems,' he would say, 'no one can give you a solution.'

The faculty had to evolve its own syllabus in personnel management, in medical and psychiatric social work, in family and child welfare and urban community development. To provide students with scope for practical work, the School started a Child Guidance Clinic in 1937 and a Community School in the Worli labour area to provide field practice in community organisation.

Except for those who had taken a course in personnel management, those who had taken the diploma in social work had difficulty in finding employment until the 1950s. With the five year plans, there was an explosion of government activity in social welfare, and the avenues for social workers thereafter widened and varied.

The early 1940s at the School were difficult because the locality of the Neighbourhood House was the scene of frequent trouble during communal riots. Professor Panakal recalls that none of the students dared to go out alone after dark and even during the day, at times of communal disturbances. Students had seen people slashed or stabbed.

Even so, the Neighbourhood House had its lighter touches. One day a pet antelope, belonging to Manshardt's son, leapt over the compound wall and started down the principal

Antelope in burqa

street of the neighbourhood. A posse of men joined in the chase to catch the antelope. At the other end of the street, a Muslim gentleman was walking down carrying a white *burqa* which he had probably collected from the laundry. In his excitement, he waved the white garment before the approaching antelope. The antelope, even more excited, charged into the garment. For a few moments the neighbourhood was treated to the spectacle of what appeared to be a white-*burqa* clad woman speeding down the street, and at intervals taking almost incredible leaps into the air.

There was a flood of activity in the early years of the School. The faculty engaged itself not only in instruction and organisation of social services but also in the education of the general public in matters related to social welfare. The faculty created an awareness of problems and a sense of urgent need to tackle them. A series of public lectures was held on the relation of various sciences to social work. The press carried scores of articles by Dr. Kumarappa bringing awareness to the Indian public, on a professional basis, of the social needs of India. He gave a series of broadcast talks under the title 'Have You Thought of Them?' He spoke on 'Where City Workers Dwell', 'Labourers' Homes—Picture of Squalor', 'Bad Housing and its Effect on Social Behaviour'. Editorials followed in *The Evening News of India* and other papers on conditions in the slums and other similar subjects.

Dr. Manshardt had also written and spoken widely. In 1940, *The Illustrated Weekly of India* had carried for a number of weeks articles by Manshardt or Kumarappa on penal reform, juvenile delinquency, the Hindu woman and desertion, and on how to prevent family disintegration. Manshardt himself published two books between 1937 and 1938. *Some Social Services of the Government of Bombay*, he edited, with contributions from senior government officials in the field of labour and social welfare on subjects like workmen's compensation, factory law, rural reconstruction and cooperative societies. The second, *The Child in India*, is an authoritative work by him, the first on this subject.

From June 1940 this small pioneering band of writers on social problems launched the *Indian Journal of Social Work*. It was inspired with the same spirit of dedication that directed their practical work in the field. The journal has served as a forum for the faculty and students of the School (and later the Institute), reporting on research studies and significant advances in social work, and has been a focal point for social workers scattered all over the country. It was not long before the journal was recognised internationally as a leading one in the field.

Thus did this pioneering group contribute, beyond all proportion to its numbers, to the social education of a nation.

In Kumarappa's time there were twelve teachers. For six days of the week they had to conduct four classes a day, bring out a journal and other publications and do a considerable amount of public relations in a country where social science still was in its infancy. 'We were a small institution with big men,' a past student recalls.

As the first institution of its kind in India, the School had to depend for a faculty on training its own people and sending them abroad for higher studies. So, when promising young men or women came along, it was Kumarappa's job to send them, after initial training, for studies overseas which would equip them to join his faculty on their return to India. This is what he did for Dr. (Miss) Gauri Banerjee, who pioneered medical and psychiatric social work; Dr. Kamla Bhoota, who trained in family and child welfare; and Professor N. F. Kaikobad, who after his Master's degree at Pittsburgh started teaching community organisation. L.S. Kudchedkar who took his degree in personnel management in London even gave some lectures in London and Oxford as a student and later became head of the Department of Personnel Management. It is the School of Social Work that had all these persons trained for their future careers. In the 1940s, with the assistance of two Americans, Miss Blakey and Dr. (Miss) Sweeney, the teaching of medical social work and child welfare were introduced. Dr. Walter Reckless from the USA was invited as a Visiting Professor in Criminology and Correctional Work. J.J. Panakal, a student, who showed a keen interest in the subject, was sent to the United States for higher training in criminology and came back as one of the first Indians to qualify in the subject. A couple of decades later, Panakal was on several committees dealing with prisons and correctional services in India.

Kumarappa felt the need to give the School a wider base to cover the whole field of social sciences, and though two or three of the Trustees were doubtful at the time, the name of the School was changed in 1944 to the Tata Institute of Social Sciences (for convenience referred to as the TISS).

During Dr. Kumarappa's tenure the Institute outgrew its premises at the Neighbourhood House and was transferred to two bungalows at Andheri, a Bombay suburb. The School, however, continued to keep in close touch with the Neighbourhood House but it may be recognised that the substitution of 'School' by 'Institute' and the physical move away from the pressing realities of hectic Bombay to the

Tata Institute of Social Sciences

peace and quiet of the suburbs could also represent a shift from the practical to the academic.

In the late forties it was realised that, to fulfil its role in the nation's life, the Institute needed suitable permanent premises of its own. Two acres of land at Worli, Bombay, were purchased by the Governing Board. However, keeping in view the potential for growth of the Institute, it was felt this would not be enough. A much larger area was acquired at Chembur, the north-eastern extremity of Greater Bombay. The move to Chembur was initiated by Naval H. Tata, who devoted a good deal of his time and energy to implementing the scheme. 'We were used to such cramped premises that when we first moved into Chembur we thought the place was too large,' said Professor Kaikobad, 'but Tatas had foresight.'

At Chembur, what was once a farm became the site of a remarkable piece of architectural design with sharp but pleasing lines.[2] The architects were G.M. Bhuta and Durga Bajpai, a pupil and a disciple of the eminent Scandinavian architect, Alvar Aolto. Even over four decades after its construction, students of architecture visit the Institute to observe the admirable use of rough-hewn stone in its design. Today, stately royal palms, breadfruit trees and other varieties of flora embrace the Institute with a lushness of greenery. A Professor of Criminology, Dr. Panakal took a great deal of interest in creating this setting.

Prime Minister Jawaharlal Nehru was invited to open the new campus on October 6, 1954. 'The moment I arrived here,' he said, 'I was pleased with the external appearance of these buildings. It is attractive, it is unusual and it seems to fit in with the type of work it is meant to do.' He recalled how the government asked the help of the Institute's workers to cope with the refugees when they streamed in after the Partition and that they 'helped us enormously'. He added,

---

2 The Sir Dorabji Tata Trust met most of the capital cost equivalent (in today's terms) to over Rs. 1 crore, with modest contributions from the Government at the State and Central levels and the Sir Ratan Tata Trust.

Convocation at the Tata Institute of Social Sciences

'we found the difference in their work and the work of many others who were earnest and had done their best but who did not have the training to do it well. There is a difference between the trained workers and the merely enthusiastic workers.' The student batch Mr. Nehru referred to had been led by Dr. Behram Mehta.

Mr. Nehru said that to him the fundamental requirement of social work was 'a feeling of community, a sense of being in tune with others.' When some students were going abroad to study social service he had asked them to serve at Gandhiji's ashram in Sevagram for a few months, saying that they would learn more that way. Techniques, observed Nehru, are important but more important is 'the human quality of the individual, the human approach, your understanding of the entire environment in which you have to work.'

In the years to follow the Institute attracted foreign students, and social scientists from the Tata Institute were also invited to teach at foreign universities like the Thammassat University in Bangkok. Others were selected for responsible assignments by the United Nations.

It was due to Dr. Kumarappa's effort that strong financial support came from the Central and the State governments, but a year before the building opened, he had stepped down as Director due to failing health.

Status of a University

The search for a suitable successor to Dr. Kumarappa was a long one. It was Dr. John Matthai, Chairman of the Governing Board, who proposed Professor A.R. Wadia, a distinguished educationist-philosopher, for the post. The choice, though unconventional since Professor Wadia was neither a social worker nor a social scientist in the formal academic sense, was a happy one, and he served the School as its Director for nine years with great distinction.

A.R. Wadia had taken a Cambridge tripos in moral sciences. From 1916 to 1942 he was Professor of Philosophy at the

Mysore University, contemporaneously for some years with Dr. S. Radhakrishnan. He was President of the Indian Philosophical Congress in 1954. It was under his guidance that the Mysore University introduced the first undergraduate course in sociology in India. He came to the Tata Institute after serving as Pro-Vice-Chancellor of the Baroda University and, while he was still at the Tata Institute, was offered two Vice-Chancellorships to run concurrently, which he declined so that he might devote all his time to the School which had become very dear to him.

Professor Wadia established a good rapport with the students who realised that, in spite of his strictness and his disciplined ways, he was an understanding Director who cared for their well-being. He conferred upon the Institute some of the dignity and the honour that the nation conferred upon him as a distinguished academician and administrator. He was awarded the Padma Bhushan. Like Kumarappa, he was also a member of the Rajya Sabha for 12 years.

With the launching of the First Five Year Plan in 1951 the demand for social workers in general and rural social workers in particular grew sharply. The government naturally turned to the Tata Institute for help. A Social Education Organisers Training Centre was established at Himayatnagar, Hyderabad, by the Union Government with the Director of the Tata Institute as its Honorary Director. The Tata Institute ran it for the Government for the first three years, got it functioning smoothly, and then withdrew.

In the 1950s, with the encouragement of the Home Ministry and the Commissioner for Scheduled Castes and Tribes, the Institute set up a Department of Tribal Welfare headed by Dr. Behram Mehta. Chhindwara district of Madhya Pradesh became a major field-work area where students of the Institute spent as many as five months in a year. Much constructive work was done, but as the Institute found it difficult to conduct a field-work centre so far away from Bombay, the Institute ultimately withdrew from the area, leaving it to local organisations to carry forward the projects that had been initiated. For field training, a cluster of six villages in the Thane District just north of Bombay was taken in hand. This project was conducted by the newly started Department of Urban and Rural Welfare under Professor Kaikobad.

Professor Wadia, as a member of the University Grants Commission (UGC), endeavoured to bring to the Tata Institute the status of a university and in 1964, two years after Wadia had stepped down as Director, the UGC deemed the Tata Institute a university.

In 1946, ten years after the TISS was founded, the National YWCA (later the Delhi School of Social Work) started. In 1950 the Baroda University Faculty of Social Work was established and in 1952 the Madras School of Social Work. As noted earlier, today there are 66 reputed schools of social work in India.

Professor Wadia was succeeded by Dr. Madhav S. Gore, till then the Principal of the Delhi School of Social Work. Dr. Gore, after qualifying at the Tata Institute, had obtained a Ph.D. from Columbia University. Essentially an academician, it was his aim to give the Institute an academic standing worthy of the status of a university. To this end he undertook greater formalisation of the curricula and programmes of the Institute. He also took steps to strengthen and widen the research base. Before Dr. Gore, there had been a certain informality in its instructional programmes, which had certainly contributed to the Institute's strength, but which could, he felt, become a liability. Previously the student was left to draw his own lessons from his field work. Dr. Gore ensured that a supervisor helped him to evaluate his work. These trends in the initial years of Dr. Gore's stewardship were strengthened when, in 1964, the UGC deemed the Institute a university. With this recognition the flow of funds increased.[3] The activities of the Institute were expanded with

---

3   While the allotment to the Institute for the 4th Five Year Plan from the UGC was only Rs. 16 lakhs, for the 5th Plan the grant was raised to Rs. 50 lakhs.

full-time research units,[4] the development of the doctoral work and the undertaking of more short-term courses than attempted previously. A considerable extension of the library also took place. Till university status was acquired, the ultimate responsibility for the financing of the Institute was that of the Trust, with the Central and Maharashtra governments making their contributions. Later the University Grants Commission took on the principal financial responsibility, with the Dorabji Tata Trust making an annual contribution.

'What difference does it make to the Institute to have this continued association with the Dorabji Tata Trust?' Dr. Gore was asked. He replied, 'I know of several institutions and I am on the Board of some of them which are cent per cent run by the government. They are always subject to the immediate whims and political demands of the ministries. Every three years the secretary of the department changes, and soon after the Head of the Institute builds up a working relationship with him, the secretary is transferred. At this Institute, in 18 years I have had to deal with only two Chairmen of the Board who were from the Trust.... The Institute would lose a good deal if the Chairman of the Board was ... just a government appointee. For me the last two decades have been a very creative and gratifying period.'[5]

When the Institute felt the need for a unit in rural studies the Dorabji Tata Trust gave an immediate grant of seed money, so that there was no delay in getting started, pending the UGC grant coming through. By giving seed money and launching a unit, the Trust provides the government with an opportunity of checking the feasibility of a project before sanctioning public funds.

---

4 The research units were devoted to studies of children and youth, the sociology of education, social policy and social welfare administration, urban studies and, later, rural studies.

5 Dr. Gore retired in June 1982 and a year later was appointed Vice-Chancellor of the Bombay University.

The Institute's contribution to the formulation of a policy in the field of social welfare has been substantial. The Director and many of his senior colleagues have served on policy-making bodies like the National Police Commission, the Bonus Review Committee and the Jail Reforms Committee. High-ranking government officers regularly participate in seminars organised by the Institute.

The performance of the Institute was reviewed by committees appointed by the Governing Board in 1952 and 1973 under the chairmanship of Dr. John Matthai and Dr. Malcolm Adiseshiah respectively. Dr. Matthai, a former Finance Minister of India, happened to be the Chairman both of the Dorabji Tata Trust and of the Board of the TISS at the time of his review. Dr. Adiseshiah, M.P. (Rajya Sabha), was formerly Deputy Director-General of UNESCO.

On the advice of the Matthai Committee, the Trust made funds available for the Institute's publishing programme. On the recommendation of the Adiseshiah Committee the Dorabji Tata Trust sanctioned a grant spread over a five-year period, to enable the Institute to organise refresher courses for rural workers. This was in anticipation of the sharp emphasis on rural welfare work in government policies and programmes that was to follow within the next two years.

The Trust has encouraged support for the creative and constructive initiatives of the TISS. Its role in providing broad-minded and far-seeing leadership to it, is a continuing one.

Chapter 5

Soiled Hands and Open Hearts

Adevastating cyclone hit Andhra Pradesh in 1977. The receding waters of the tidal wave carried away tens of thousands of helpless men, women and children, in addition to cattle, into the Bay of Bengal. The news reached the rest of the country in the morning. The same afternoon the Trust sanctioned an initial sum for a small relief group from the TISS. That night they set out by train for the scene of the calamity. When the team arrived they discovered that they had to deal not only with the material damage caused by the cyclone but also with the despair of the people who had lost their loved ones as well as their belongings. To resuscitate the spirit of the people is as important as to reconstruct homes and meet their immediate needs for food and health care.

Where death and devastation had dampened the spirits of the local people, one evening the TISS team dared to sing Hindi film songs. The spirit caught on. Government officials touring the area were quick to recognise the difference between the work of the TISS volunteers and other agencies. 'For the first time,' government officials said, 'we have met here a group that can sing.'

In one village only four children had survived. Three were given slates and pencils and sent back to school. The only art the stricken women knew was basket-weaving. 'But who will buy them?' they helplessly enquired. The students assured them a market in Vijayawada. The government was giving assistance of Rs. 1000 to the next of kin of each adult who had perished. The students liaised with the authorities to ensure that the money came. Moneylenders quickly came forward to collect dues. The volunteers sought to protect the villagers.

Dr. M.S. Gore, Director, TISS, insisted that such emergencies are no excuse for postponement of the

Relief work after the cyclone

examinations. 'Whatever we are doing should not be at the cost of what we are expected to do. The TISS is a university and its prime function continues,' the Director said.

A good part of the practical side of social work is not as spectacular or short-term as relief work. Nearer home, the TISS Child Guidance Clinic was opened more than 40 years ago. Most parents who brought their children then complained about stealing, lying and truancy. Today's problems are somewhat different. Life has become so competitive that, when children do not fare well at school, parents get much worried. They do not accept the fact that their child may be below the average and keep pushing him or her into more competitive schools which may finally break the child. A parent's pressure lowers the child's performance and the job of the clinic is often to help the parents to let go of their ambitions. Institute students join the Child Guidance Clinic every week to assist and learn practical techniques.

A typical case is that of a 6-year-old boy called Karim. His father was a young man of 36. The child was withdrawn, the father was strict. Karim was constantly corrected and scolded. He stammered more in the presence of his father than when alone with the clinic worker. Mental testing revealed that the child's IQ was 117, his grasping power good, and he could concentrate on a given task. The father did not permit Karim to go out of the house to play because he picked up bad language from his friends. The excessive strictness of the father had to be tempered. He was helped to see the futility of beating Karim. These efforts led to a reduction in Karim's stammering and relaxation of his neck muscles. And there was a noticeable change in his speech; he no longer dragged his words.

The next step was to encourage the father to be a friend to Karim and to spend some time with the child. To create a relaxed atmosphere at home, it was suggested to the father that he might like to ask Karim to sing and perhaps sing himself. Gradually the father and son began to enjoy each other's company. Four months later, the father reported that he did not notice any stammer in Karim's speech when he spoke. The clinic worker met Karim occasionally for a check-up over the next couple of months. Then, the Karim case was closed.

Drugs, Curiosity and Boredom

An interesting survey was undertaken in the early 1970s on the use of drugs in three Bombay colleges. The findings revealed that the major factors that prompted students to take drugs were curiosity and boredom. While friends could prompt young people to experiment with drugs, other friends also contributed to inhibiting the students from resorting to drugs. Four-fifths of the students interviewed had never tried drugs. Only in the case of the high income group—where the family income was Rs. 3000 and above per month—did the percentage of drug-takers rise to 84 per cent.

Matrimonial Counselling

In 1979 the Matrimonial Judge of the Bombay City Civil Court made an unusual request. He asked whether the TISS could run a Matrimonial Counselling Service at the City Civil Court. It is one of the functions of the Matrimonial Judge to reconcile partners whenever there is a chance, but the pressure of legal work does not usually permit a judge, however eager he might be, to spend the time and energy needed for this work. Therefore, Mr. Justice H. Suresh made this request to the TISS. The Dorabji Tata Trust made a one-time allocation for the launching of a matrimonial counselling service at the City Civil Court which would assist not only in the reconciliation of couples who sought a divorce but also, when reconciliation was not possible, with settling the problems of care and custody of the children and alimony with the minimum of bitterness. They also helped the estranged partners in coping with the emotional problems that grow out of disharmony at home. This Matrimonial Counselling Unit, the first of its kind in the country, is now funded from another source. Its success may well lead to its multiplication in the rest of the country.

Fresh Avenues

Dr. Manshardt spoke of the conflict between academic social scientists and social workers who undertake practical field work. Dr. Gore sees no such conflict. He sees both as part of social service. As Director till 1982 he wanted to see the TISS enlarge the concept of social service to embrace issues of health, education, housing and rehabilitation. Professor

N.F. Kaikobad, former Head of Rural and Urban Community Development, TISS, and later an expert with the UN, believes that, so pressing are the problems of India, that research and action must be closely linked and that perhaps future research should, at the same time, be a quest for a solution to a problem. This may involve a research team of two working on a problem and the solution, one essentially an academic person and the other a pragmatic field worker.

The Institute has so far completed some 550 research projects, either on its own or under the sponsorship of other agencies. Among those who sponsored research and other academic programmes are: the Union Education Ministry, the Union Welfare Department, various departments of the State Governments, the University Grants Commission, the Indian Council of Social Science Research, the Tata Trusts and many industrial concerns, the UNESCO, UNICEF, ILO, FAO, Ford Foundation, Oxfam and others.

At any one time more than 80 urban and rural research projects are in various stages of their initiation or completion. The range of researches vary from basic to applied to action to evaluative studies; their orientations vary from diagnostic to policy prescriptive, from quantitative to qualitative; and the substantive areas are predominantly the socio-economic and welfare dimensions of problems that concern our country.

As the first and premier Institute of Social Sciences, it has one of the finest libraries in the field with 87,600 volumes. It subscribes to 371 journals. Acquisition of books and journals have been badly affected in recent years due to a cut in the budget by the University Grants Commission. The TISS has been publishing the *Indian Journal of Social Work* uninterruptedly for over five decades, a track-record perhaps unrivalled by any other social science journal in India. The publications department has over 60 books to its credit.

To ensure that the Institute is in touch with the latest techniques, it has its own Audio-Visual and Electronic Data Processing Units, which are undergoing further sophistication.

The original name of the Institute, the Sir Dorabji Tata Graduate School of Social Work was changed to the Tata Institute of Social Sciences in 1944. From the 1960s greater emphasis was put on social science by its then Director Dr. M.S. Gore. Eight research units were formed over the next decades including one on urban and rural studies.

The Institute's contribution extends way beyond the training of its own students. It organises scores of special courses for training of officials of the IAS, the Indian Police Service, the Indian Forest Service and other services and organisations. The staff of the Institute works on policy-making bodies like the National Police Commission and the Jail Reforms Committee, Commissions for Women, and, helps to provide the inputs the policy-makers need. After a significant contribution to building the College of Social Work — Nirmala Niketan, Dr. (Ms.) Armaity S. Desai became Director of the TISS in 1982.

A Ph.D. of Chicago University and a former student of the TISS, Dr. Desai combines the ability to build and run institutions with an intense concern for the well-being of individuals. This writer has met individuals with very humble backgrounds who testify to that. A Christian gentleman, janitor of the building in which Dr. Desai resided, spontaneously spoke of Dr. Desai's guidance in educating his children and finding jobs for all of them; a housemaid on how Dr. Desai sorted out her marital complications and cared for her children. Along with this, she can undertake with zest practical field work. When the earthquake struck Latur District in Maharashtra in 1993 she was on the way to the site within 30 hours with some emergency material and a small team. In a couple of weeks she had every single student of the TISS involved in relief work or taking a census of casualties which the Government requested the TISS to do. It was an enviable field experience under her leadership. The prompt and daring steps she took during the Bombay riots of 1984 drew admiration.

In February 1995 when she completed 12 years as Director,

the Prime Minister appointed her as Chairperson of the University Grants Commission. She was called upon to apply her talents on the wider canvas of the Indian nation.

At the TISS she inherited from her predecessor Dr. Gore a solid foundation of social research. In turn she gave the Institute a thrust at the field level concentrating on the poor and the disadvantaged to develop strategies for their well-being. The field action projects she initiated include:

1. Children: child labour; street children; co-ordination among agencies providing child welfare services and day-care.
2. Women: marital conflict, desertion, divorce and family violence. The Institution runs two cells in Bombay, including one at the Police Commissioner's headquarters, to help women who are battered, maltreated or thrown out of their homes.
3. Tribal development.
4. The growing malaise of drug addiction.
5. Rural development.

With the growing emphasis on rural development the government was keen to tap the expertise of the TISS to train rural workers. The Government of Maharashtra gifted 100 acres of land in Tuljapur, Osmanabad District, which was on barren land and bereft of trees or of water. The first venture of the TISS was to green it. Even before adequate buildings can come up, numerous activities relating to land and water management, social development, women's empowerment and education, have been taken up in the neighbourhood of Tuljapur (Osmanabad District). Activities are extended through training programmes, direct intervention and collaboration with the government and other NGOs. The geographical purview sometimes extends well above Osmanabad, into the whole of Marathwada region. The Ford Foundation recognising its potential gave a grant of 156,000 US dollars as seed money to establish the Rural Campus. Since the crucial drought years in the early nineties, the Rural Campus has addressed itself to watershed development and community orientation towards irrigation management.

After 40 years at the Bombay Campus, the shortage of space was seriously affecting the functioning of the Institute. The hand of fortune intervened and 10 acres of land almost next door to the Campus were willed by Mrs. Malati Jal Naoroji. Her late husband, a grandson of Dadabhai Naoroji, was a Director of Tatas. The Sir Dorabji Tata Trust Trustees in March 1995 sanctioned one of its largest single grants of Rs. 3.25 crores for the development of campus buildings in Bombay and Tuljapur.

In some ways an Institute of this nature has to provide not only a training ground but also to function as the social conscience of a nation.

In March 1995 Mr. J.J. Bhabha stepped down as Chairman of the Governing Board, having held that position for 25 years and Mr. B.G. Deshmukh, IAS (Retd.), former Union Cabinet Secretary and later Principal Secretary to the Prime Minister, took over as Chairman.

On March 1, 1996 Professor Partha Nath Mukherji joined as the new Director. A Ph.D. from Patna University, his doctoral research was on *Sarvodaya-gramdan* movement. Subsequently, as the *Bhoodan-gramdan* movement waned and the Maoist agrarian movement surfaced with intensity, he researched extensively on the Naxalbari peasant uprising in West Bengal. Thereafter, he made a macro-study of rural labour in the States of Haryana, Uttar Pradesh and Bihar, studied the farmers' movement in Punjab and the ethnic movement of Gorkhaland. Professor Mukherji, who began his teaching career in 1963 in the Post-Graduate Department of Sociology, Patna University, has also taught in the Delhi School of Economics and the Jawaharlal Nehru University at New Delhi. He joined the Institute, after a 16-year spell as Professor of Sociology, at the Indian Statistical Institute, first at Calcutta and then at New Delhi. A close associate of Jayaprakash Narayan he is influenced by Gandhian values.

The Tata Graduate School of Social Work has come a long way since its Nagpada days. Starting some sixty years ago as a neighbourhood institution, it has today international status. Nevertheless, there is no scope for complacency. Tumultuous changes are rocking the country and the world. It is necessary to grasp these changes and the consequences they spell for our people, particularly the vulnerable sections of our society — the deprived, aged, women, disabled and children in order to grapple with them effectively. Ecological and environmental degradation threaten the healthy survival of humankind. The Tata Institute of Social Sciences is poised to address these new challenges with originality, innovativeness and determination in its research, teaching, training and field action projects. It is in this constant preparedness of the Institute to rise to the challenges of changing times in the service of the nation the Founders' dreams will find fulfilment and vindication.

Part III

TATA MEMORIAL CENTRE

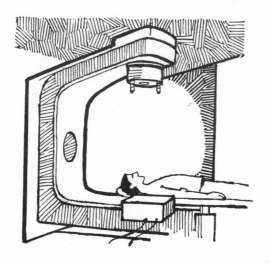

Chapter 6

A Labour of Love

Whicheimr Lady Meherbai Tata died of leukaemia—cancer of the blood—Sir Dorabji, who always had an interest in the fight against disease, was stirred to do something about the treatment of cancer. Just at that moment, Sir Frederick Sykes, Governor of Bombay, discussed with Sir Dorabji a plan to establish a radium service in the city. As originally envisaged, the scheme was for the purchase of 400 mg of radium and an endowment for its upkeep. Sir Dorabji told the Governor that his past experience in dealing with the government in regard to benefactions had not been happy but he was agreeable to financing the project. Details were being worked out when Sir Dorabji died in June 1932.

In 1933, Sir Dorabji's secretary, N.M. Muzumdar, made a fervent appeal to the Trustees to do 'something out of the ordinary which the average run of philanthropy does not touch or cannot reach; something with a future ....' as a memorial to Sir Dorabji. He strongly urged persistence in the radium institute project and support to quinine research, in which the Trust was also interested. In the Trust's minutes of September 27, 1933, it is recorded that Sir Nowroji Saklatvala, on board an ocean liner on the Pacific, met Dr. John Spies. Dr. Spies happened to be the Head of the Cancer Service of the Peiping Union Medical College of the American University in China. He had earlier worked at the Sloan Kettering Memorial, New York, one of the foremost cancer institutes in the world. Sir Nowroji mentioned to Dr. Spies how the late Sir Dorabji Tata had thought of assisting in the establishment of a radium institute in Bombay. He invited Dr. Spies to India to report on the proposal.

Dr. Spies was invited to meet the Trustees on August 23, 1935, in Bombay. He recommended 'a small but high-grade institution', with 50 or 60 beds to begin with, to be increased up to a 100 or 150-bed hospital in course of time. In his report, he said:

> The best interests of the cancer patient demand that all effective methods of treatment be made available at one place, so that a judicious choice of a well-considered combination of methods may give to such a patient his best chance of a cure, or failing that, his best chance of life and the relief of pain.

Sir Nowroji was eager to launch on a comprehensive cancer institute. In this he was supported by J.R.D. Tata who, along with the auditors, was asked to make an estimate of the Trust's assets and annual income. This was necessary if the Trust was to undertake a major long-term financial commitment. Sir Nowroji felt that a cancer hospital was well within the capacity of the Trust to support. 'The Trust,' he said, 'had already the wherewithal and sinews with which to proceed.' The next two months were months of debate and discussion in the Trust on the nature of the institution to be set up—whether only for radium treatment or for full-spectrum treatment; only treatment or training and research also. The broad project had been approved but the details needed careful working out. It was considered advisable to seek the opinion of the Curie Institute, Paris, on Dr. Spies' report.

By December 1935, Dr. Spies (rather prematurely) was already writing to various experts round the world in the hope of putting them on the payroll considerably in advance of any of the other plans proceeding. He was also planning to send nurses abroad for training. By 1936 it was estimated that the initial expense on the hospital would be Rs.11 lakhs* with an annual expenditure of Rs. 2 lakhs. On November 13, 1937, Sir Nowroji was reporting to the Trust meeting: 'Our hospital budget has gone up out of all proportions. Naturally Dr. Spies wants to put up the hospital on a very modern scale which requires serious thought.' Sir Nowroji said that the earlier estimate of the Trust's income worked out by the auditors in

---

* Value of the Rupee 1 lakh equals to Rs. 83 lakhs of 1997.

collaboration with J.R.D. Tata was too rosy. Sir Nowroji observed:

> We would say that things are looking up now but we cannot take that position as a basis for all time. From the figures you will notice that we [the Dorabji Tata Trust] have got to depend mainly on the Tata Iron and Steel Company and on Tata Sons and I would, therefore, ask you to take these figures with some caution. Another point I would emphasise is that the strength of the Trust is the strength of the Tata firm. Sir Dorabji anticipated it and under the Trust Deed has allowed the firm to use a certain amount of fixed deposits and this is the safeguard for the Trust as for the firm. I am, therefore, very reluctant that money should be spent up to the hilt in carrying out an ideal scheme.

The Trustees now had on their hands a hospital project of dimensions much larger than any private organisation in India had till then taken on entirely on its own; it had no precedent from the Suez to the Sea of Japan; and the field was highly specialised. The Trustees were mainly men of industry, men who knew the nuts and bolts of steel manufacture but nothing about radium, X-rays or cancer. There were many pulls and pressures on them as they screened every little detail from the nurses' call system to air-conditioning equipment.

It was in these circumstances that Dr. Clifford Manshardt, who, as was noted in an earlier chapter, had already advised the Trust on its programme, was requested to undertake the duties of Director of the Trust, primarily to help in the execution of the cancer hospital project. Anticipating the needs of the project, he advised that the Trust foreign scholarships should, for some time, be restricted to scholars who were going abroad to train for the cancer hospital—surgeons, radiologists, pathologists, dieticians and nurses. Years later Manshardt was to record:

> I directed enquiries to all the leading cancer centres in the world and eventually produced a preliminary report on the project. The Managing Trustee of the Trust at that time was Mr. J.D. Ghandhy— a man over eighty years of age, but mentally alert as a man of forty. Mr. Ghandhy was keenly interested in the subject of cancer. I remember one day in his office when a committee of Bombay doctors

advised us against undertaking the radium project on the ground that it was too difficult, Mr. Ghandhy turned to me and exploded: 'Difficult? Did Jamsetji Tata ever quit because of difficulties? We will go ahead!'

Clifford Manshardt continued:

Only those who were associated with the hospital project during the years of its planning will ever know the amount of hard work that went into the making of the Tata Memorial Hospital. Only those who shared in the ups-and-downs, the disappointments and successes, can realise the human anguish that went into the institution. As a layman, I had been inclined to idealise the medical profession, but long before my education in medical politics had been completed, I realised that doctors engage in the same kind of feuding that is found in less exalted professions. It is true that American professional consultants, without adequate knowledge of Indian conditions, did make errors of judgement in respect to organisational details of the hospital, but strong nationalistic feelings on the part of a group of Bombay doctors, who had considerable influence with the Trustees, did not make the task of arriving at a working mean any easier. An undertaking of the magnitude of the Tata Memorial Hospital would have been difficult in any country, but to rear an institution of this

Tata Memorial Hospital

kind, in the face of the limitations under which we were working in Bombay, required imagination, energy, patience, pertinacity and obstinacy.

Just as the scheme was finally getting off the ground, the sudden death of Sir Nowroji Saklatvala in Europe in 1938 stunned the Trustees. In the following months they had naturally to devote themselves almost wholly to adjustments in the various business enterprises with which they were connected. The affairs of the hospital had to wait. 'The vitality seemed to drain out of the hospital project for a time,' Dr. Manshardt has recorded, 'and it was with the greatest difficulty that its momentum was restored. But finally, after many delays, caused in considerable part by the outbreak of the Second World War, the hospital was completed.'

The hospital was opened on February 28, 1941, by the Governor of Bombay, Sir Roger Lumley. There, for all to see, was the magnificent seven-storeyed structure. It had been thoughtfully designed and structured for its utilitarian purposes. Well lit, bright and airy, it had taken exactly four

years to complete. The site, formerly marshy and
water-logged, had to be drained before excavation. The
choicest material was used in its construction; the best
possible equipment had been procured from round the world,
though it was wartime. The capital grant by the Trust for
the totally equipped hospital was over Rs. 31 lakhs equivalent
of Rs. 23 crores of today. In his Foreword to this book,
J.R.D. Tata recalls his intense participation in the designing
of this Hospital.

'What has impressed me most,' said Sir Roger Lumley, 'is
the greatness of the conception, and the care and the patience
with which it has been worked out. There has been no tinkering
with the problem.' About the donors he said:

> The name of Tata is known throughout the world as a House of
> great industrialists and as a family of great philanthropists; but of all
> of the philanthropic projects connected with that name, none would
> attain a greater importance, or reflect greater credit on its founders,
> than the Tata Memorial Hospital for cancer.... This Hospital is the
> first large contribution of India to the international fight against
> cancer.

The Chairman of the Dorabji Tata Trust, Sir Sorab
Saklatvala, observed that the Tata Memorial Hospital was
meant to be a temple of learning, where doctors and research
students would work 'to wrest from this dreaded scourge some
of its terrible secrets.' 'The Trust,' he said, 'had the good
fortune to command resources sufficiently large to enable the
hospital to be constructed and equipped on a generous scale.
Each department of the 90-bed hospital bore witness to the
infinite care lavished on every detail':

> Today we confront you with the fruits of 5 years of unremitting
> work . . . this monumental undertaking represents a labour of love
> . . . it is a task in which many men have faithfully laboured, inspired
> with the hope that in doing so they set their hands on a project
> which may well spell happiness and good health to many millions of
> their fellowmen.

The architectural features of the hospital were designed, and
the construction was supervised, by the firm of Gregson,

Batley and King. It had operating theatres, lecture theatres, and all the necessary facilities, including those for research. Professor Regaud of the Curie Institute and Dr. James Ewing of the Sloan Memorial, New York, were the two experts who played a great role in advising the hospital. Dr. Spies seems to have dropped out of the scene fairly early on and it was a Dr. Van Allen who handled purchases abroad. The two top surgeons when the hospital opened were Dr. John Poole and Dr. Roy Cohn. Dr. Poole, who came from the Sloan Kettering Memorial Hospital, was a meticulous surgeon. Dr. Cohn was a typical product of a tough medical school, the Massachusetts General Hospital, a part of the University of Harvard.

Nine months after the hospital opened, the US entered the War against Japan in December 1941 and both surgeons were called back to the US Armed Forces. Dr. Cohn left a year after the hospital started. Poole continued for two more years. The Dorabji Tata Trust had in the meanwhile ensured the training of four young Indian doctors who, within three years of the opening of the hospital, were in total charge of the surgical side: Dr. J.C. Paymaster, Dr. E.J. Borges, Dr. D.R. Meher Homji and Dr. D.J. Jussawalla. The Department of Pathology was headed by Dr. V.R. Khanolkar and of Radiology by Dr. K.P. Mody. Among the senior administrators was Col. Sir Jamshed Duggan. With very few exceptions, like the two top surgeons, the staff of the hospital from the start was entirely Indian. Three years later it was totally Indian.

Freshly returned from training abroad, the four young Indian doctors soon found their former professors of surgery watching them perform complicated cancer surgery for the first time in India. It is a measure of the dedication of these four young surgeons that they devoted the rest of their working careers to the Tata Memorial Hospital, for which purpose they had been trained. They spurned many a lucrative opportunity to work abroad.

In 1968, ironically, cancer struck back at Dr. Borges. When doctors operated to investigate, they found the disease had spread too wide to be arrested and they closed the incision.

As soon as he could get on his feet, Dr. Borges worked unperturbed for another six weeks operating on other patients.

The following two weeks he was immobile. Those were his last. The disease he sought to fight in others had claimed victory over himself, as happened to Father Damien in his battle against leprosy.

Death need not have been proud .... Dr. Borges' funeral was scheduled to leave his home at 11.30 a.m. but crowds of former patients and their relatives thronged at his residence to pay their last tribute to a man they loved. Only at 3.30 p.m. could the funeral procession start.

At the condolence meeting one speaker quoted a saying which summed up Dr. Borges' philosophy of life:

I shall come this way but once.
Therefore any good I can do let me do it now.
For I shall not pass this way again.

Homi Bhabha Rescues Hospital

From 1941 to 1948, the Trust ran the hospital entirely on its own. In 1949, the Bombay Government sanctioned an annual donation of Rs. 1 lakh.* Seventy-five per cent of the beds were free and the Dorabji Tata Trust had poured into this Hospital Rs. 1 crore by 1957. The amount was huge for those days.** However, it is not so much the money that had been poured in as the concept and its successful execution which is most commendable. Dr. D.J. Jussawalla, who now has an international standing as a cancer specialist, says that had the Dorabji Tata Trust not started the cancer hospital it would have been another 15 years or more before the government could have undertaken a project of this dimension.

---

* Rs.20 lakhs of today.
** Contribution was made between 1937-1957.

By 1957, the Trust realised that the demands on the hospital were enormous. The Trustees had to choose between holding down its growth or seeking assistance for expansion. This, they felt, could come on an adequate scale only from the government and in April 1957 the hospital was handed over to the nation. The Union Ministry of Health took charge. With its multifarious commitments and responsibilities, however, the Ministry of Health was unable to provide the means needed for its sustained growth. In fact, the standard of even the routine functioning of the hospital started declining because of financial constraints and bureaucratic delays.

Dr. Homi Bhabha was told of this sad state of affairs by Dr. Paymaster and Dr. Jussawalla. The latter urged Dr. Bhabha to get the Tata Memorial Hospital made the responsibility of the Atomic Energy Commission, pointing out that the US Atomic Energy Commission ran a number of cancer research hospitals. Dr. Bhabha approached the then Prime Minister, Jawaharlal Nehru, and requested him to transfer to the Indian Atomic Energy Commission the running of the Tata Memorial Hospital.

'What, Homi!' said the Prime Minister, 'You now want to run a cancer hospital? I am not so sure you should, but go ahead if you feel it is necessary.'

Dr. Bhabha spelt out for Jawaharlal Nehru how the US Atomic Energy Commission, concerned about radiation, ran some cancer research hospitals in the US. Nehru gave his assent.

This decision saved the hospital. On its Board, since 1963, came outstanding men like Dr. Homi Bhabha, and, later, successive Chairmen of the Atomic Energy Commission, like Dr. Vikram Sarabhai and Dr. H.N. Sethna. They brought to the hospital not only their experience and the prestige of their office, but also the considerable resources that were available to the Atomic Energy Commission. Though today great demands are being made upon the services of the hospital, the Atomic Energy Commission tries its level best to undergird it with funds year after year. The Tata Memorial budget for 1995-1996 was Rs. 31 crores.

In 1966 the Tata Memorial Hospital and the Indian Cancer Research Centre were merged into the Tata Memorial Centre with the Chairman of the Atomic Energy Commission as the Chairman of its Governing Council, the Dorabji Tata Trust having three representatives on the Council and helping to steer the Centre.

Magnet or Catalyst?

Although there are about 15 cancer hospitals in India today, the Tata Memorial takes the brunt of about one-third of the total number of cancer patients treated at these hospitals. Increasingly, the authorities of the Tata Memorial have been feeling that the Hospital should act as a catalyst rather than as a magnet. Hence there is a growing emphasis at the Tata Memorial on training doctors from other regions in every aspect of cancer treatment, so that they can return to their areas with new skills and know-how.

At any given time there are 15 to 20 medical professionals, scientists and technicians from all parts of the country training in different divisions of the Tata Memorial Centre. Some 70 to 80 post-graduate students from the Centre do their Master's or Doctorate with the Bombay University, making it a large post-graduate training centre. Whenever help is required anywhere in India to start a cancer hospital or a cancer wing in a general hospital, the Tata Memorial makes its know-how available.

One cancer hospital which the Tata Memorial assisted in starting was the Meherbai Tata Memorial Hospital in Jamshedpur, named after Sir Dorabji's wife. This too started with a seed grant from the Sir Dorabji Tata Trust, though later it is donations of Tata companies like Tata Steel that lifted this hospital to its present status. Today it is acknowledged by the Union Government as a research centre for cancer in Eastern

India. It serves not only the community of Jamshedpur but patients from the crowded region that is known as the 'Ruhr of India.' The man who has shaped it over the years was a radiologist called Dr. K.D. Reddy.

Cancer has to be fought on many fronts. The first is prevention; the second is early diagnosis; the third is treatment; and the fourth is research. Cancer, caught at the early stages, is often curable or controllable. Eighty per cent of cancers in India are in the Head and Neck region, oesophagus, the lung, the cervix or the breast. Seventy-five per cent of the cancers that come to Tata Memorial are in the third or fourth stage, which makes their cure more challenging. The present Director of the Tata Memorial, Dr. (Ms.) Dinshaw estimates that 30 per cent of cancers can be preventable as they are mainly due to lifestyles. A change in our habits will prevent a lot of suffering.

The success of the Tata Memorial and its repute come from the fact that it is one of the largest comprehensive cancer centres in the world. Its 441 beds make it the largest in Asia and the Middle East. Its Cancer Research Institute is also the largest institute for basic research in cancer in this part of the world.

One of the Trust representatives on the Board was Farrok S. Mulla, a founder of the Public Relations Society of India. In 1970, Mulla sensed some abdominal discomfort, had it promptly checked and was operated for cancer. In 1973 he had a second operation. Past 70, the last ten years of his life he spent two days each week helping with the running of the hospital, using his experience with other patients. The Tata Memorial had given him a new lease on life — twice over. He in turn gave back to the Tata Memorial what he could contribute, until the cancer finally overtook him.

Chapter 7

New Life for Old

For persons suffering from cancer there seems to be magic in the name 'Tata' and there are times when doctors at the Tata Memorial Centre wish that the magic was not there. Although there are many other cancer hospitals in India – four in New Delhi alone (and many other general hospitals have separate cancer wings), patients stream to the Tata Memorial Centre, Parel, Bombay, from as far as Kashmir and Kanya Kumari in India, from the Gulf, Pakistan, Afghanistan and the countries of Africa. They arrive at odd hours at the hospital, some after a long fruitless search for a cure. They come to the gates unannounced, their eyes bespeak their hopes for admission and a cure. The facilities are stretched to the very limit.

Cancer incidence is relatively low among Indians, but cancer of certain parts of the body is more common here than elsewhere. There is a high incidence of oral cancer, pan chewing and smoking habits being the high-risk associated factors. Regional variations are also seen: cancer of the palate in coastal Andhra Pradesh, oesophagal cancer in Gujarat, abdominal and cervix cancer in southern parts of the country, and lip cancer in Bihar.

Lip cancer in Bihar is observed to be associated with the habit of keeping a quid of tobacco with lime at the inner side of the lower lip. As a large percentage of cancer in India occurs in easily accessible body organs, there is the possibility of easy and early detection.

Statistics show that while in Connecticut, USA, an average of 329 males per 100,000 persons suffer from cancer, the corresponding figure for Singaporean Indians is 93; in Bombay city, 69; and in Alibag, just across the harbour from Bombay, 43. Even allowing for the more complete registration of cases in Western countries than here, India is still found to be less vulnerable to this dreaded disease than Western countries. Nevertheless, cancer is not a disease of modern civilisation as some may think. Even on 3000-year-old well-preserved Egyptian mummies cancerous growths have been diagnosed. Modern civilisation accentuates the disease; but it also enables us to identify it and, hopefully, control and cure it.

From the moment a patient hears he or she has cancer, the effect is one of shock both to the patient and the family. The whole tenor of their lives can get seriously upset. Even though 70 per cent of patients at the Tata Memorial Centre are treated free, if the wage-earner is the victim, finance is a major problem. If the disease is arrested, there is the matter of rehabilitation or, often, finding a job for one of the family members, if the head of the family is immobilised.

Cancer treatment is expensive for an average Indian. A first-rate cancer hospital has to give comprehensive care, beginning with every form of treatment from chemotherapy through radiotherapy to surgery—and the doctor has to care enough to keep in touch with the patient for the rest of his or her life. There has to be a continuing link between the patient and the hospital and as many as 500 old patients turn

up at the Centre each afternoon for a check-up or treatment, even years after they have been cured initially.

Each day, the Tata Memorial Centre gives radiation therapy to 6000 patients annually, the largest number in any hospital in the world. The equipment used included Cobalt Beam units and the more modern Linear Accelerator from the US that enables deeper penetration of the beam and ensures that there are no 'side-reactions' that normally accompany radium treatment. Each unit costs Rs. 75 lakhs plus. The Tata Memorial Centre's staff of 2,750 looks after a daily average of 1,000 out-patients, including the 450 patients who come in for radiation therapy, and the 441 in-patients.

Not only old people are affected by cancer. Even children are sometimes afflicted—in the majority of cases by cancer of the bones, eyes or blood (leukaemia).

Shabnam Hussain is 2½ years old. Her mother is the most cheerful of parents in the children's ward. She says: 'The doctor is very pleased with Shabnam's progress and tomorrow we will be discharged to go back to Bangladesh where we come from. We have no cancer hospital there and no drugs are available for chemotherapy but my relatives will supply the drugs from abroad.' She hopes to return to her job as Assistant Professor of Geography but she has to keep in close touch with her child's doctor at the Tata Memorial. 'Any time I need help, I am told I can come back.'

Sadder than Mrs. Hussain's case is Mrs. Shah's. She has a haunted look as she tends her nine-year-old son, one of whose legs has been amputated because of bone cancer, and the doctors have told her that they will have to do the same to the other. There is a cupboard full of attractive toys donated by patients. A child may play and, in a better moment, even laugh. A child's pain may be relieved by drugs but who can assuage the suffering in a mother's heart as she sees one leg of her child amputated and then is told that the same will happen to the other? Doctors, social workers and nurses need something more than just technical competence to work in a cancer hospital.

One day in 1969 Abdul Majid Ayub from Kashi (Varanasi) turned up at the hospital. He had a painful swelling in the mouth, under the right cheek. He had drifted from Kashi to Ahmedabad and from Ahmedabad to Baroda in search of a cure, till he finally landed at the Tata Memorial. During the many months he wandered in search of a cure, his 12-loom mill in UP was mismanaged and misappropriated by relatives. He was in debt when he arrived in Bombay. At the Tata Memorial he was operated and his gaping wound closed with plastic surgery.

It is usual for a social worker to interview those who go back to the mainstream of life after treatment; Ayub was interviewed and sent to the Rehabilitation Centre not far from the hospital. Here he was tested by a psychologist and an occupational therapist and was invited to impart his skills in weaving to other patients who needed rehabilitation. In the last 12 years Ayub has worked at the looms and trained scores of former cancer patients, some of whom have gone out and found jobs in mills. He has called his family to Bombay, paid all his debts and had his two daughters married. He says that when he goes back to his *mohalla* in Kashi everyone marvels at seeing him fit and thinks of the hospital in far away Bombay. His cure and subsequent rehabilitation have prompted 50 more from his town alone to come for treatment to the Tata Memorial. 'I earn Rs. 750/- here. Friends invite me to return to Kashi and say that they will help to re-establish me. in business and that I can make much more money there. But I am useful here to others in need and I can pay back the debt I owe to society.'

The Rehabilitation Centre is not run by the Tata Memorial Centre but was established by the Indian Cancer Society founded by Dr. D.J. Jussawalla (a former Director of the Tata Memorial). It helps, in a most valuable way, to supplement the activities of the Centre and makes cancer services in Bombay the most comprehensive anywhere in India.

Mr. Zed from Assam came to the Tata Memorial with cancer of the larynx. Operated at the age of 28, he could not speak and wanted to end his life. He was shown how people could speak without a larynx by forcing air through the oesophagus, using belching to produce sound. First he had to be persuaded to try this method and he picked it up in a couple of weeks. Now in Assam he has trained about 90 former cancer patients to speak in this fashion and he has even spoken on All India Radio, Calcutta. 'It is not enough to add years to life, it is important to give life to the years added,' is the motto of the Rehabilitation Centre. The less skilled work on the manufacture of simple articles like toothbrushes; the more skilled may even fix switchgear equipment. A US government agency gave a Rs. 9-lakh grant for four years. Its skilful utilisation enabled 232 patients and their families to earn Rs. 4.75 lakhs a year, proving that it pays to put money into rehabilitation.

Several years ago a dedicated team of father and son called Nene, both doctors, asked Tata Memorial for help in starting a rural cancer project. Confident of their dedication, Tata Memorial offered them help and sent their best doctors to assist with the project at Barsi, Solapur, including the then Director, Dr. Praful Desai.

It is with this strong support that India's first rural cancer project came to birth. Their mobile van tested people for cancer. Prevention is better and cheaper than cure.

On the occasion of the Golden Jubilee of the establishment of Tata Memorial, Sir Ratan Tata Trust, in an imaginative gesture decided to give substantial support to this project. Within five years, complicated procedures could take place at Barsi. Tata Memorial gave the technical support, Sir Ratan Tata Trust gave the final thrust, but it was the dedication of the local doctors that made a success of this financial enterprise.

*   *   *

Cancer is a resolute adversary for any patient. Thanks to the modern treatment, if detected early most cancers are either curable or controllable. Certainly people have longer longevity with modern medicines than they ever had before. For example 30 years ago chemotherapy was in its infancy. Today, along with surgery and radiation it is a major weapon in the treatment of cancer. However there are times when cancer can neither be cured or even controlled and patients diagnosed as 'terminally ill', in which event only care is possible. To give such care, love and compassion along with a modicum of medical attention, a surgeon at the Tata Memorial Hospital, Dr. Lusito J. de Souza launched in the early 80s his idea of starting a Hospice for the 'terminally ill'. With great devotion and with the co-operation from all sectors and especially the Catholic church which released its prime land opposite Mount Mary Church, Bandra, India's first centre for terminally ill cancer patients was created.

Located on the top of the hill facing the Arabian Sea, the Home is so designed that the patient can have a view of the sea from every bed. A view of the sunset over the waters is particularly inspiring. Catholic sisters of the Order of Holy Cross have devoted their lives to run this home call Shanti Avedna which means (abode of peace).

The strain on the sisters running these homes is exceptional. To give personal care they give their hearts to the patients and in 48 hours, 72 hours or even a few weeks the patient is no more. The result is that every few months sisters have to take a break due to emotional exhaustion, revive themselves and return.

One senior gentleman of Mumbai, Prof. M.P. Gandhi read in the first edition of this book about Sir Dorabji Tata Trust starting the Tata Memorial Hospital in the memory of Lady Tata and he approached Mr. J.R.D. Tata for advice on how he could commemorate the memory of his wife who too had died of cancer. He was directed by the author to Shanti Avedna and he donated a ward in the memory of his wife. Years later when Shanti Avedna set up another home in Delhi he gave another handsome donation once again in the memory of his wife. Dr. de Souza has also started a home in Goa and is a pioneer in the field whose work was recognised and he was decorated with the Padma Shree. However his greater satisfaction lies in the gratitude of those who in the sunset of their lives can watch the sun peacefully slip away over the waters of the Arabian Sea.

For those last days and hours, the patient is cared for. 'I have known terminally ill women of even 70', says Dr. de Souza 'who once their pain is relieved, want to live on.' 'What we start can become a nationwide movement,' he says.

*   *   *

Within the precincts of the hospital complex is located the Radiation Medicine Centre (a division of the Bhabha Atomic Research Centre) and the Cancer Research Institute. At the Cancer Research Institute ten divisions specialise in studying different aspects of cancer. The main thrust of the research is on prevention. Nearly 30 per cent of cancer may be prevented. That is why the Cancer Research Institute also studies different lifestyles, food and other social habits.

Cancer is an aberration or abnormality of the body's own normal processes. A certain regulatory mechanism controls normal cell growth in our bodies. When this regulatory mechanism goes haywire, the normal restraint on the growth is removed and you get an abnormal multiplication of cells. One aspect of cancer research is to turn back cancerous cells into normal cells.

The Indian Cancer Research Institute was established in 1952 with the renowned pathologist, Dr. V.R. Khanolkar in charge. He was a man of great vision and undertook research in cell biology and tissue culture, when both these subjects were in their infancy. Today, intense research is being done at the Tata Memorial Centre into various types of leukaemia and lymphoma. For these studies, the Lady Meherbai Tata Trust provides some additional funds for research projects. For studies in leukaemia the Lady Tata Memorial Trust makes available to an international experts committee in London funds for research projects in leukaemia and related fields. A sum of pounds 200,000 sterling was sanctioned in 1994-95 to ten scientists from different countries. On a smaller scale scientists and institutions within India are also given grants.

Christopher Columbus set out for India and ended up in America. The Indian Cancer Research Centre set out to cure cancer and finds itself on the brink of a major breakthrough in leprosy treatment. In 1958, under Dr. Khanolkar, a bacillus, named ICRC, which has many antigenic similarities with leprosy germs (*M. leprae*) was isolated and cultured from patients of lepromatous leprosy. Such patients harbour massive numbers of germs and lack immunity against them.

In 1978, under Dr. M.G. Deo, the work took a new direction. An anti-leprosy vaccine was developed from gamma irradiated ICRC (Indian Cancer Research Cells) bacilli, which had been isolated from human leprosy patients and grown in culture. Growing these bacilli in culture was a major breakthrough. A large scale trial was launched in 1987 in the south-eastern part of Maharashtra to evaluate the protection given by the vaccine to such contacts. This part of the country has prevalence rates of leprosy as high as between 8-10 per 1000. About 35,000 healthy household members of leprosy patients were vaccinated. They will be followed for 10 years to evaluate protection given by the vaccine.

It is generally seen that a small fraction of leprosy patients who are given multiple drugs do not respond to the treatment. The bacterial counts in such resistant patients were reduced when they were given vaccine along with drugs and there was a general improvement along with increase in their immune responses. A new clinical trial is now being started to test the efficacy of the vaccine as supplement to multi-drug therapy.

The Cancer Research Institute has focused its research on cancer which are more frequent in our country. The major cancers in men of the mouth cavity is due mainly to the widely prevalent tobacco and smoking habit. In chronic tobacco chewers, a small white patch called 'leukoplakia', develops on the cheek which in some cases progresses to a cancer. Scientists at the Cancer Research Institute (CRI) whose Director since 1995 is Dr. A.N. Bhisey, have undertaken research work on the changes in genes associated with development of cancer in these tumours and the pancreas.   Such studies in future may help develop a test for earlier diagnosis.

The CRI scientists have been in the forefront of research using modern tools and techniques in molecular biology. One of the areas where the Institute has initiated work is gene therapy of cancer which aims either at correcting a basic change in a tumour cell or introduce a 'suicide' gene in tumour cells to kill them. The Cancer Research Institute scientists have chosen the second approach and are developing techniques of suicide gene therapy for treatment of oral cancer. Scientists are also studying the immune mechanism that can destroy the oral tumour cells. The aim is to boost the patient's immunity against these tumours. Similar studies are being carried out on cancers of breast and uterus.

Considering the role of tobacco in the development of cancer, scientists at the Institute have pioneered programmes for assessing the risk to which tobacco and *bidi* industry workers are subjected by carrying appropriate tests on them. The scientists have also isolated the deadly HIV virus – which causes AIDS – from the Indian patients and have developed a reliable but much less expensive diagnostic test.

Until such time as effective means are found to cure cancer, prevention and early detection will continue to be of utmost importance. 'Almost 40 per cent of cancers in India occur in the oral/pharyngeal region (compared to only 7 per cent in the USA) and this is entirely because of our habits,' says Dr. Praful Desai, Director of the Tata Memorial Centre, 1980-95.   He goes on to add that if these habits are given up, in 25 years we will be able to see a definite decline.

Youthful in appearance and absorbed in his job, Dr. Praful Desai says that 25 years of cancer surgery 'has changed my attitude to life, because now I understand how beautiful life is. Because I have seen death at very close quarters, I have also learnt to live life very intensely. I don't know what's going to happen in the future. Tomorrow I may have cancer. Anyone of us can have cancer.... That's why I know how productive life should be.'

In 1995, after a distinguished directorship, Dr. Praful Desai retired. Dr. R.S. Rao, who had served the hospital for 32 years became Director of the Tata Memorial Centre for a short while. Dr. (Ms.) Ketayun Dinshaw, a Radiation Oncologist qualified in England who had served Tata Memorial for 21 years took over as Director of the Tata Memorial Hospital and thereafter also of the Tata Memorial Centre. She was nominated President of the International Society of Radiation Oncology for 1997-98.

*   *   *

To relieve the pressure on the hospital, the Dr. Borges Memorial Home was developed at Bandra, a suburb of Bombay, to house up-country patients who have to visit the hospital for radiotherapy and chemotherapy. Free transport is provided for the patients. They do not need to occupy precious space at the hospital nor search for accommodation elsewhere. Nearly 150 out-of-town patients make use of the facility during their stay in Bombay for treatment. It has served a great human need.

Tata Memorial's greatest problem is over-crowding. For its Golden Jubilee (1991) the Atomic Energy Commission financed a huge Annexe at the rear of the existing two buildings. Apart from enabling better patient care the new building houses facilities for services like cancer prevention, education and screening of high-risk population. A new out-patients department and an ultra-modern auditorium for academic meetings are an important component of the new buildings for Tata Memorial in the front line of cancer education in India.

The current bed strength at the Tata Memorial Hospital has risen to 441 and the budget through the Department of Atomic Energy is Rs. 30 crores. In the last 15 years the area of activity has increased from 36,591 sq.m. (1980) to 53,387 sq.m. (1994). On the occasion of the Golden Jubilee, 70 outstanding cancer specialists of the world participated in Seminars and Workshops at the Tata Memorial Hospital providing a stimulus not only to the staff of the Centre but young professionals from all over the country.

In 1990, the Tata Memorial Hospital spearheaded and succeeded in the bid to get the prestigious international event (16th International Cancer Congress) to India and the Tata Memorial Centre played host to the Congress in October/ November 1994. Within a week of the conclusion of this major Congress, the then Tata Memorial Centre Director, Dr. Praful Desai, was planning a new Complex for comprehensive cancer treatment, research and training on a 60-acre plot in New Bombay which would be comparable to any in the world.

The new complex of the Advanced Centre for Treatment, Research and Education in Cancer (ACTREC) will be commissioned by 2000 A.D. in a phased manner and in the early years of the 21st century. When the complex at Vashi, New Mumbai, is totally completed, it may become perhaps one of the world's first universities entirely devoted to education, treatment and research in cancer. It hopes to attract many Indian cancer specialists now abroad to return home providing them adequate facilities for research and treatment.

Over the last years bone marrow transplant operation has given new life to many. It is a moving experience to meet those who have survived over the last years. One of those who underwent this operation at Tata Memorial Hospital is Annapurna in her twenties. She said: "I am so happy, I want to live here and be here." Doctors Advani, Tapan and Purvish Parikh who are primarily responsible, pass on the credit to specialised nursing sister Ms. Mohite because it is the nursing care and the hygienic standards which ensure that bone marrow transplant patients survive.

When asked if Tata Memorial keeps in touch with the bone marrow survivors, Dr. Advani replies emphatically: 'It is they who keep in touch with us although we follow up. We are like a family.' That is a bond that is knit between a patient whose life is saved and the doctor and the institution that saves it.

In 1997 a state-of-the-art CT Scan machine was installed. It makes available three dimension pictures to a surgeon at the operation table or a radiation doctor for therapy. Such facilities of modern science are possible because of the interest of successive chairmen of the Atomic Energy Commission who are also Chairmen of the Tata Memorial Hospital. The Atomic Energy Commission keeps Tata Memorial in the forefront of cancer treatment and research.

Part IV

TATA INSTITUTE
OF
FUNDAMENTAL RESEARCH

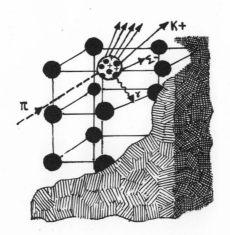

Chapter 8

Dr. Homi Bhabha – Vision and Creation

Human progress has always depended on the achievement of a few individuals of outstanding ability and creativeness. Homi Bhabha was one of them.

Sir John Cockcroft

On August 8, 1928, a young Indian of 18 was writing from Cambridge to his father in Bombay:

> I seriously say to you that business or a job as an engineer is not the thing for me. It is totally foreign to my nature and radically opposed to my temperament and opinions. Physics is my line. I know I shall do great things here.

Homi Jehangir Bhabha was pleading with his father to allow him to switch from an engineering to a mathematics tripos. Father and son struck a bargain. If Homi got a first class in engineering, he could do two years more of mathematics at Cambridge. In June 1930 Homi obtained a first class in the mechanical sciences tripos and thereafter went to work as a research student in theoretical physics and passed out first class with a tripos in mathematics.

The first years of his research work coincided with a remarkable period at the Cavendish Laboratory, Cambridge. In 1932 Chadwick demonstrated the existence of the neutron; Walton and Cockcroft achieved the transmutation of light elements by bombardment with high-speed protons; and Blackett and Occhialini demonstrated by beautiful cloud chamber photographs the production of electron pairs and showers by gamma radiation. It was a period of great interest and excitement in the world of theoretical physics. Homi was selected to an Isaac Newton Studentship in 1934 and travelled

Photo: Yousuf Karsh

to the principal European centres of theoretical physics. He studied at the Niels Bohr Institute of Theoretical Physics in Copenhagen, the Mecca of theoretical physics; with W. Pauli in Zurich and with Enrico Fermi in Rome.

From the age of 17 to 29 Homi Bhabha studied and worked in the West and nowhere in the world could he have found a finer atmosphere for his study than in Cambridge in the 1930s. With two exceptions, Bhabha's papers at Cambridge were written by him alone. A mathematical physicist, he lectured at Cambridge from 1935 to 1939. For him it was a fruitful period. In a paper he published in 1937 Bhabha and Heitler enunciated the celebrated Cascade Theory of Cosmic Ray Showers.

Cosmic rays are particulate matter, such as atomic nuclei and electrons which move with great energies in the spaces between the stars of our galaxy. These radiations from outer space strike the earth and their study is of great relevance to nuclear science and astronomy.

In 1939 Homi Bhabha published two important papers. One reported the existence of a hitherto unknown fundamental particle in the penetrating component of cosmic radiation. The second gave the quantum theory of this particle which has since been called the Mu-Meson. The first paper explained the production of 'showers' by the penetrating component through the agency of 'collision electrons'. The process was named after Bhabha. All these 'great things' he achieved before he was 30. He also found at Cambridge the time to design and paint sets for plays and operas as well as to paint and draw for his own pleasure. He was fond of track-running and tennis.

At the age of 30, Bhabha came on a holiday to India. While he was here, World War II broke out and he was unable to return to Cambridge. In 1940, through a special grant from the Sir Dorabji Tata Trust, he was appointed Reader at the Indian Institute of Science at Bangalore, and two years later he became Professor of Cosmic Ray Research. The five years he spent in Bangalore were important years in his life in many ways. Professor M.G.K. Menon, who succeeded Homi Bhabha as Director of the Tata Institute of Fundamental Research (TIFR) said: 'I believe this was the period when he found his mission in life; he became aware of the role he could play in the development of India.'

As Bhabha contemplated at Bangalore on issues concerning the development of the country, the inadequacy of scientific facilities in India came sharply into focus. On August 19, 1943, he wrote in a letter to J.R.D. Tata that 'lack of proper conditions and intelligent financial support hamper the development of science in India at the pace which the talent in the country would warrant.' He mentioned that he himself had had an idea of accepting at the end of the War a job at Cambridge or Princeton but had come to the view that, provided proper facilities are available, 'it is one's duty to stay in one's own country' and build up schools comparable with those in other lands. Mr. Tata replied:

> If you and/or some of your colleagues in the scientific world will put up concrete proposals backed by a sound case, I think there is a very good chance that the Sir Dorabji Tata Trust... will respond. After all, the advancement of science is one of the fundamental objectives with which most of the Tata Trusts were founded, and they have already rendered useful service in that field. If they are shown that they can give still more valuable help in a new way, I am quite sure that they will give it their most serious consideration.

The Dorabji Tata Trust had not only provided the money for the establishment of the Cosmic Ray Research Unit at the Institute of Science, it had also provided, in the 1940s, at the request of Jawaharlal Nehru to J.R.D. Tata, a cyclotron (an apparatus used to accelerate subatomic articles) for Professor M.N. Saha, the well-known scientist at the Calcutta University.

It became clear to Dr. Bhabha that fundamental research in physics and mathematics, including nuclear physics and cosmic rays, was too big a subject to be dealt with in a small department of a university or in a general purpose research institute. It needed an institution devoted primarily, if not solely, to this end. With this conviction, reinforced by the encouragement of Mr. Tata, Dr. Bhabha wrote, on March 12, 1944, a formal letter to Sir Sorab Saklatvala, Chairman of the Sir Dorabji Tata Trust. In this letter, which he wrote at one sitting, he described his vision for the India of the future. '... when nuclear energy,' he wrote, 'has been successfully applied for power production, in say a couple of decades from now, India will not have to look abroad for its experts but will find them ready at hand.' Closing the letter he said:

> The scheme I am now submitting to you is but an embryo from which I hope to build up in the course of time a school of physics comparable with the best anywhere. If Tatas would decide to sponsor an institute such as I propose through their Trusts, I am sure that they would be taking the initiative in a move which will be supported soon from many directions and be of lasting benefit to India.

When Bhabha spoke of nuclear energy at that time, he was not aware that work on the atomic bomb was already far advanced and that 18 months later the world would awaken to the first atomic blast at Hiroshima. All that he knew was that nuclear fission (the splitting of the atomic nucleus) had been achieved and his mind was already engaged in working out means for its use not for destruction but for the generation of electric power.

Nearly two decades later, in a report to Jawaharlal Nehru, the Prime Minister, Dr. Bhabha was to observe: 'My proposal was considered by the Trustees of the Dorabji Tata Trust in the light of two covering notes on Trust policy written by the Director, Professor R.D. Choksi. The first note entitled, "Note on Trust Policy", which I saw for the first time a few days ago, gives an admirable and clear statement of the objectives of a big Trust.' This note has already been quoted in Chapter 2 (p. 28). Professor Choksi's second note dealt specifically with Bhabha's proposal:

> A further reason for advocating full support to Dr. Bhabha's scheme lies in the pioneer character of the undertaking. The Trust has always stood for pioneer work. It undertook a project in the field of Social Sciences in 1936, it completed and established a much

larger project in the medical sphere in 1940, and in 1944 it may well enter upon a modest project in the field of pure science. It is important that the Trust should maintain its character for pioneer work.

While the Trustees were debating this issue on April 14, 1945, Dr. Bhabha was waiting in the anteroom. Though elsewhere there may have been discussion on whether a poor country like India could afford the luxury of 'pure' research when there were such pressing economic problems before it, the Trust accepted J.R.D. Tata's view that fundamental research was necessary and the point to decide was whether the Trust could take on such a commitment stretching over a period of years—which involved launching another major institution.

The minutes of the Trust record:

> After discussion of the financial implications of Dr. Bhabha's proposal as embodied in his letter, the Trustees decided to undertake the responsibility. They were of the opinion that this responsibility should be shared from the outset with the Bombay University and the Bombay Government—both in respect of finance and administration. It was remitted to Professor Choksi under the general direction of the Chairman to explore the possibilities of such cooperation with the University and the Government. Dr. Bhabha was present at this stage of the meeting and entered into the discussion. He readily accepted the Trustees' views regarding the sharing of responsibility.

Thus the Trust took on the responsibility both in terms of long-term finance and administration for the new institute. J.R.D. Tata tried to interest a senior industrialist friend in supporting the project. In a letter to him dated June 22, 1945, Mr. Tata spelt out his vision of what this Institute could do for the country:

> I sincerely believe that this Institute can make a great contribution to the scientific knowledge of mankind . . . You may perhaps feel that advanced physics, mathematics, astrophysics, are particularly abstract subjects, research in which is unlikely to produce material or practical results within a reasonable period of time. I should, however, like to point out that most of the great practical advances

in science, and therefore, in industry, have had their origins in fundamental research, without which they would have been impossible or would have been long delayed.

Although nuclear physics is today still in the realm of pure science, physicists already believe that within a relatively short period of time this branch of physics will make available to man a new, immense, and inexhaustible source of motive power. Thanks to the work done in this field by Bhabha and some other Indian scientists India has already contributed her full share to the present day knowledge of the subject. More than ever before, the future of modern civilisation will depend on scientific progress, and that progress itself will continue to depend on pure research. Because the realisation of this is becoming universal all the important countries of the world have enormously increased the extent and scope of their activities in pure research, and India should not be allowed to lag behind in this vital quest for knowledge. She has men of world renown, like Homi Bhabha, Chandrashekhar and others, and if given proper facilities she is more than capable of holding her own.

Circumstances prevented the industrialist from associating with Tatas in this great project, but, fortunately, for the new Institute the initial Tata grant of Rs. 45,000 per year (the equivalent of about Rs. 14.5 lakhs in 1997) plus the Rs. 25,000 of the Government of Bombay was augmented by a grant from the Government of India of Rs. 10,000, a combined total of Rs. 23 lakhs of today. The University of Bombay did not join in but the interest of the Union Government at an early stage was an encouraging sign. The Union Government's block grant the next year was as large as the combined contribution of Tatas and the Government of Bombay. From then on, the Government of India bore considerable financial responsibility as it valued the work of the Institute. The credit for this goes primarily to Dr. S.S. Bhatnagar who, in 1947, became Director-General of the Council of Scientific and Industrial Research and was at the same time Secretary to the Ministry of Natural Resources and Scientific Research.

Dr. Bhabha believed that while the government should support scientific institutions financially, they should not be placed under government control. Under its constitution, the TIFR is run by a governing council on which the Sir Dorabji Tata Trust, the Government of India, the Government of Maharashtra and, latterly, the Atomic Energy Commission are represented. The Department of Atomic Energy now provides the funds for running the Institute.

When the Sir Dorabji Tata Trust had sanctioned the proposal, Sir Sorab Saklatvala, Chairman of the Trust, became the first Chairman of the TIFR with a provisional committee consisting of Dr. John Matthai; S.N. Moos, Director of Public Instruction, Bombay Presidency; and Dr. Homi Bhabha. On June 1, 1945, the Institute began functioning in Bangalore as Dr. Bhabha and his facilities were based there. However, Dr. Bhabha always felt that the Institute should be located in Bombay and by December 1945 it had already shifted to an old bungalow, 'Kenilworth', on Peddar Road (now Dr. Deshmukh Marg) owned by his aunt, Miss Cooverbai Panday.

Kenilworth

Half of that old house, about 6,000 sq.ft. was obtained on a rent of Rs. 200 for Dr. Bhabha to instal his little laboratory and staff. Inaugurating this first home of the TIFR on December 19, 1945, Sir John Colville, Governor of Bombay, said: 'We are embarking on an enterprise of importance to the country's development, in which great wealth, wisely husbanded and applied, individual initiative and government support are all blended. I do not think there could be a better combination for progress.'

Professor Kosambi, the well-known mathematician was one of the first to be invited to join. N.R. Puthran, a young accountant, joined the Institute when it had a staff of six. He recalls that Peddar Road in those days had gracious bungalows with hardly a couple of buildings more than two storeys high. Homi's aunt was very fond of her nephew and Homi was always served tea in the finest chinaware of the house. The nearest teashop was at Gowalia Tank, half a mile away, and for the convenience of the then small TIFR

Yacht Club

family, Miss Panday allowed the use of her staff and kitchen to serve their refreshment needs. On Parsi New Year's Day, the TIFR family feasted on traditional Parsi delicacies. Miss Panday's warmth and kindliness pervaded the Institute and made them all feel that they were really part of a family.

The Institute soon outgrew these small premises and one day the building had to be vacated for demolition. Mr. Puthran recalls that, on their last day there, Homi's mother, Meherbai, came to 'Kenilworth' and nostalgically recalled that the room on the first floor, where her son had worked as Director, was the very room in which he was born. Puthran, who worked with Bhabha for the next 20 years, recalls that in all those years, he cannot recall Homi Bhabha ever losing his temper or raising his voice. He gave so much of himself that all those who worked with him felt they had to do the same.

Dr. Bhabha enjoyed the good-will and unquestioned confidence of the Trustees as he was later to enjoy that of

Prime Minister Nehru. Sir Sorab Saklatvala told the accountant: 'Cheques and other routine papers should be put up to me for signature so that Homi can spend his time on scientific affairs.' Dr. John Matthai, one of India's most distinguished administrators, assisted Bhabha in the formulation of administrative norms.

In September 1949 the Institute moved into the picturesque 35,000 sq.ft. premises adjoining the Gateway of India previously occupied by the Royal Bombay Yacht Club.

The premises was bought by Tatas when the British left India for an extension of the Taj Mahal Hotel but the policy of prohibition then introduced proved a deterrent to the Hotel's expansion.

In 1962, as described later in this chapter, they moved to their present premises in the south-east of Bombay overlooking the Arabian Sea, and the old Yacht Club became the head office of the Atomic Energy Commission.

In its early years, the Institute concentrated on mathematics and theoretical physics. The experimental work was in cosmic rays and high energy particles.

Bhabha, the theorist, had earlier started experimental cosmic ray studies in Bangalore, flying his instruments high in planes of the US Air Force. He was inspired by the studies R.A. Millikan had earlier carried out in India. It was clear to him that research in modern experimental areas was of the utmost importance, for its own sake and also to provide the right balance for theoretical studies. Experimental work generated confidence in the design, fabrication and use of equipment.

In 1948 the Atomic Energy Commission was formed with Bhabha as Chairman and in 1954 the Atomic Energy Department of the Union Government with Bhabha as Secretary. These offices he held concurrently with the Directorship of the Tata Institute which he was busy developing. However, he clearly demarcated the respective roles of the Atomic Energy Establishment (AEE) which was coming up at Trombay (Bombay) and the TIFR. The functions of the AEE (later the Bhabha Atomic Research Centre—BARC) was to undertake research of a technical or semi-technical nature, aimed at solving problems arising in the design and construction of atomic reactors. The TIFR was to undertake research in all aspects of atomic science without reference to immediate utility. As Bhabha said:

> The TIFR can carry out its largescale projects of fundamental research. Fundamental research thrives best in an atmosphere that is free, permitting an unrestricted exchange of ideas. An institution for fundamental research should be open to all scientists of eminence, whatever the country to which they belong, and should be unfettered by the secrecy regulations required in commercial or strategic establishments. Had the Institute (TIFR) not existed, the Indian Atomic Energy Commission would have been compelled in time to create such an institution where fundamental research in atomic science could be carried out in a free academic atmosphere on a scale larger than is convenient in a university laboratory.

Over the years, Dr. Bhabha trained a hard core of scientific personnel at the Tata Institute. When the Atomic Energy Establishment started, he transferred 46 of them from the TIFR to the AEE, including Dr. Raja Ramanna, Head of the TIFR Nuclear Physics Group and A.S. Rao, Head of the Electronics Group. There was a time when the entire staff of the fledgling Atomic Energy Establishment at Trombay was looked after by the Institute and its administration carried on from the TIFR, which had the necessary infrastructure. It was at this time that the control system of *Apsara*, the first atomic reactor in Asia, was built under the auspices of the Institute in a wartime hutment, many parts of the reactor being fabricated at the TIFR workshop. When the Atomic Energy Training School (now the BARC Training School) was started in 1957, to train the manpower required for the growing atomic energy programme, a major part of the teaching load in the initial years was carried by the TIFR scientists. Dr. Bhabha observed:

> It is not an exaggeration to say that this Institute (TIFR) was the cradle of our atomic energy programme, and if the Atomic Energy

Establishment at Trombay has been able to develop so fast, it is due to the assisted take-off which was given to it by the Institute in the early stages of its development. It is equally true to say that the Institute could not have developed to its present size and importance but for the support it has received from the Government of India.

Dr. Bhabha was planning the expansion of the TIFR at the same time as he was working on the blueprints of the Atomic Energy Establishment at Trombay which included designing the landscaping of its gardens. Mr. D.N. Marshal, then Librarian of the Bombay University, recalls Bhabha coming to the University Library after his office work to study books on landscaping and gardening.

The Yacht Club could not serve as a permanent home for the growing Institute. Space large enough to accommodate the Institute of the future was being examined. The only land Dr. Bhabha found spacious and suitable enough was in the extreme south of Bombay in an area belonging to the Ministry of Defence. He applied for it. The Ministry of Defence, then headed by Krishna Menon, initially turned down the request. Dr. Bhabha went up to the Prime Minister and through Mr. Nehru's intervention had the land released, and started constructing on it a magnificent structure of 2,50,000 sq.ft. He was intensely involved in the architecture, design and structure of the building. The architect, Helmuth Bartsch, was to say later: 'In the past I have always worked for my clients. This is the only time I have worked with a client.' Dr. Bhabha converted what was once a site for coastal batteries into a large expanse of green lawns and a small casuarina forest extending almost to the sea front.

For Homi Bhabha, the Tata Institute was to be a 'Centre of Excellence' for the country. What put it in a class by itself was his close personal attention to every detail, be it the buildings, the gardens, the art collection, or, most important, the scientific programmes and their high standards—they all bore the unmistakable imprint of Homi Bhabha's personality and genius.

Dr. Bhabha was a lover of art and a patron of artists. He

TIFR New Building

bought scores of paintings in the 1950s and early 1960s of artists who were later to become famous — Hussain, Chavda, Raza, Gaitonde and many others. He had a sculpture of the head of Einstein fashioned by Jacob Epstein; a Rajasthan temple pillar of the 9th century A.D.; fragments of sculpture of the Chola period from South India (A.D. 10th century) which included a large Vishnu; and several wood carvings. He personally supervised the hanging of paintings and the placing of the other works of art. He was proud of the new building. Some months before it was completed, on February 28, 1961, he issued the following standing order:

> These buildings are as fine as any corresponding buildings to be found anywhere in the world and no pains have been spared in providing the members of the Institute with as good conditions of work and amenities for their comfort and general well-being as are to be found anywhere today. The buildings have been paid for by generous grants from the Sir Dorabji Tata Trust and the Government of Bombay, and above all, from very substantial grants made by the Government of India. These buildings have, therefore, been made available to the staff of the Institute by the people of India through the taxes they have paid.

> Each member of the staff should have a sense of personal pride in these buildings, which have been given for his use, and it is his duty to take personal interest in their proper maintenance and to see that he himself uses them in such a way as to maintain their quality and cleanliness and so as not to cause inconvenience to others. Certain normal and elementary good manners with regard to the use of the buildings and the fixtures and furniture in them must be observed. A member, who sees another not using the buildings properly should draw his attention to the proper conduct in such matters. If any person continues to misbehave, the matter should be reported to his superior.

> The strictest norms of cleanliness should be maintained throughout the buildings, more especially in the lavatories. Feet should be wiped on a mat before entering the building, and marks from dirty hands should not be left on the walls. Lavatories should be used properly and kept spotlessly clean.

Four years later, March 26, 1965 he issued another standing order to say that the facilities he had referred to were not being used by members of the staff as they should be and 'those who continue to behave in an unhygienic and unsocial manner will have to leave the Institute.'

Bhabha wanted to create in India something much more than a scientific institute. He wanted to establish a centre for research that would radiate to the rest of the country standards as high as any to be encountered anywhere. What is heartening is that these standards are still maintained. Thirty years later the building is as good as new.

Within six days of the approval of the institute project by the Trust in April 1944, Bhabha was inviting the renowned astrophysicist, Dr. S. Chandrashekhar, who was working in the USA, to join it. He told him that it was his endeavour 'to build up in time an intellectual atmosphere approaching what we knew in places like Cambridge and Paris.' He envisaged a day when the Institute would move beyond the immediate requirements of pure science and come closer to the humanities. At the opening of the Institute he wrote to Prime Minister Nehru:

> I have also had the idea that some day the Institute might render useful service to this country by carrying out research in the history of Indian science. If the contributions of India and the East to the progress of science in the past ages and their relations to world science are to be systematically investigated and appreciated in their proper historical perspective, it is necessary that a great deal of work on the history of Indian science should be done with the proper modern scientific and critical outlook. This is a subject which the Institute might possibly take up at some later stage, if the proper people to do the work can be found.

A beginning was made in 1957 with the TIFR publication of a facsimile edition of the notebooks of Srinivasa Ramanujan, the renowned Indian mathematician, who was elected a Fellow of the Royal Society in 1918.

Homi Bhabha's mind ranged over a wide spectrum of human endeavour—the arts, music, science and industry. Way back in 1952 he was thinking in terms of using solar energy for air-conditioning in Bombay. He was very keen that the finest foreign scientists should visit India and lecture at the TIFR and among those who came at his invitation were several Nobel Prize winners in physics, including Professors Niels Bohr, W. Pauli, P.A.M. Dirac, P.M.S. Blackett and Sir John Cockcroft.

The whole of Sunday, January 23, 1966, Dr. Bhabha worked at the TIFR and his close group of scientists and administrators worked with him. He spoke to them about his ideas for the rapid development in India of science, technology and industry.

He was to leave that night for Europe and, as was their practice, they were all present at the airport before he left in case he had last minute instructions to give. He took off for Geneva. Early next morning, as his Air-India plane, the *Kanchenjunga*, was flying over Mont Blanc, it crashed into the frozen heights of the Alps.

The following day *The Guardian*, London, wrote: 'India has lost a prophet and a guide in Dr. Bhabha who single-handedly at the start, set the nation's sights on the highest peaks of technology.' The *New York Times* recalled that only a few days earlier the Indian atomic scientist had said that India was only 18 months away from nuclear capability. The paper called the TIFR 'the biggest Indian research laboratory'. At the age of 24, writing to one of his trusted friends, Mrs. Jessie Maver, Dr. Bhabha had said:

I know quite clearly what I want out of life. Life and my emotions are the only things I am conscious of. I love consciousness of life and I want as much of it as I can get. But the span of one's life is limited. What comes after death no one knows. Nor do I care. Since, therefore, I cannot increase the content of life by increasing its duration, I will increase it by increasing its intensity. Art, music, poetry and everything else that I do have this one purpose— increasing the intensity of my consciousness and life.

The personality of Dr. Bhabha was summed up by Lord Redcliffe-Maud:

Affectionate and sensitive, elegant and humorous, dynamic, one of the very few people who enhance life whatever the content of their living .... Whatever he set himself to do, he did as a professional—but one who worked for love; restlessly creative, enhancing life because he loved all forms of it.

One of the men that Dr. Bhabha left behind to continue the atomic programme was Dr. Homi Sethna. Sethna called his *guru:*

> ... a man of outstanding dimensions, a giant among men. He was an engineer *par excellence* and a scientist, an intellectual of rare calibre, a savant of art and culture, a sensitive artist himself, and an inspiring leader and an architect of modern India. Above all he was a visionary who looked far into the future and tried to shape it .... He laid firm foundations for self-reliance in nuclear technology.

That 'firm foundation' was laid at the TIFR. During his lifetime Bhabha created the infrastructure that gave India the support for its leap into the atomic age.

What Homi Bhabha achieved for India would not have been possible without the sustained support he received first from J.R.D. Tata and later from Jawaharlal Nehru.

It was J.R.D. Tata who ensured that Bhabha's genius would flourish in India rather than flower in Cambridge or Princeton. Barely overcoming his characteristic modesty, Mr. Tata was to say about this in later years: 'Of all the activities in the creation of which I have played some role, in this case a very minor one, there is none of which I am prouder today than the Tata Institute of Fundamental Research.' It is perhaps a small but significant fact that for three successive Sundays the Chairman of Tata Sons, who also ran Air-India, came to the TIFR with Dr. Bhabha for discussing the model, design and details of an auditorium for the TIFR. This was completed only after Bhabha's death and is named after him.

Jawaharlal Nehru gave Homi Bhabha his utmost trust, support and confidence. Indira Gandhi in her speech at the inauguration of the Homi Bhabha Auditorium in 1968, disclosed that it was on board a ship in 1937 that Homi Bhabha, then only 27, met her father Jawaharlal Nehru. Said Mrs. Gandhi:

The life of a politician lacks many of those warm moments of sensitivity that other people take for granted in their everyday life .... I know that Homi Bhabha opened one such 'window' for my father, and he always found it no matter how tired my father was, no matter how late it was in the night, he always found time for Dr. Bhabha, not only because the problems which Dr. Bhabha brought were important and he wanted to give them urgent attention, but because he found at the same time it was relaxing and it was an entirely new world.

The stature of a man can be judged by the width of his mental horizon. Homi Bhabha was a man who bridged the generations— he bridged the old and the new, the West and the East. He was equally at home in the world of science and in the world of the arts. For, he was a creator and a doer—a man of thought as well as a man of action.... India owes him a very great deal. Amongst his many activities he founded this Institute of which we are all so proud, the Tata Institute of Fundamental Research.

Bhabha left a personal collection of distinguished works of art, including a Picasso, paintings of some of the finest Indian artists of whom he was a prime patron, as also an impressive array of his own paintings and drawings. The TIFR and the Bhabha Atomic Research Centre are also his legacies. Perhaps his richest legacy is in the large number of trained scientists who, alongside him, embraced the vision of a new India, confident in her ability to stand before the world.

Professor M.G.K. Menon, who succeeded Bhabha at the TIFR and later became Secretary and later Minister in the Union Ministry of Science and Technology, says:

Homi Bhabha sought to create the right environment and right conditions for work. He succeeded in enthusing those who worked around him with the same spirit of dedication in national endeavour which motivated him, enthused them to maintain the highest standards of scientific integrity, and to set standards of quality in all that they did. This viable, self-generating group of trained personnel, the scarcest commodity in a developing nation, products of Homi Bhabha's inspiring and warm leadership, are his richest legacy to India.

Much was to flow from this legacy in the years to unfold.

Chapter 9

On the Frontiers of Discovery

*The Institute's task will never end, for the frontiers
of knowledge will always lie ahead.*

J.R.D. Tata

I f Indian scientists have explored the edge of the known
universe through a powerful telescope and have plumbed the
depth of the deepest mines in the world for studying cosmic
rays, it is because of the existence of the Tata Institute of
Fundamental Research. In the fields of radio astronomy and
of cosmic rays India is right there on the frontiers of
discovery—advanced as any other nation.

On a green hillside just beyond Ootacamund in the
Nilgiri Hills is the radio telescope of the TIFR scanning the
blue skies for radio waves. On the basis of its readings,
Indian scientists are discovering fresh pulsars, fantastic space
clocks that emit radio waves at regular intervals. The radio
telescope can also determine the size and distance of other
celestial objects. India is ideally suited as a location for a
radio telescope since it lies in the equatorial region. No other
country in the region is sufficiently advanced scientifically
to conduct her own research. A National Centre for Radio
Astrophysics has been set up as part of the TIFR.

Three hundred miles further north, at Kolar Gold
Fields' 8000-foot deep mines intricate instruments are
placed in the bowels of the earth to analyse cosmic rays
which bombard the earth from outer space. How and
exactly where they originate,̈ we do not know, but they
are powerful enough to penetrate through the earth's
surface and were measured at Kolar in the second deepest
mine in the world.

From the confidence gained by designing and building the
radio telescope at Ooty, TIFR scientists are now

implementing a proposal to build the very ambitious Giant Metrewave Radio Telescope (GMRT) at Khodad, near Narayangaon, north of Pune. It would be the largest telescope in the world at these wavelengths. Again, it takes advantage of the proposed site being relatively free of background radio noise. Further, a novel ingenious design of the antenna has been evolved using a concept that has come to be called the Indian rope trick or "SMART", i.e. Stretched Mesh Attached to Rope Trusses. In Europe, where during winter the antennas have to be capable of bearing the weight of a lot of snow, such a design may not have been thought of. This telescope would be capable of tackling many important astro-physical problems such as the epoch of galaxy formation.

Since ancient times man has tried to unravel the mystery of the universe. Physicists believe that the world is made up of particles and certain forces. Particles are protons, neutrons, electrons, and so on. Forces are of four kinds: gravitational, electro-magnetic, the 'strong force' which holds the nuclei of atoms together, and the 'weak force' which makes radioactive decay possible.

Isaac Newton spelt out his theory of gravitation. Einstein too was concerned with explaining this force. Ampere, Oersted, Faraday and Maxwell gave us an understanding of the electro-magnetic force in the universe. Salam, Weinberg and Glashow, who jointly received the Nobel Prize in 1979, unified the electro-magnetic and the 'weak nuclear force'. The next step being pursued by Salam and others for a Grand Unification Theory is to link these two with the 'strong force' that holds the nuclei together. Grand Unification Theories predict that even the proton decays but it takes a long time to do so. To verify this prediction about the decay of the proton an experiment was conducted at the Kolar Gold Fields by the TIFR.

At Kolar, two or three events which could be due to such

proton decays were recorded. These observations were used to put upper limits on various proton decay modes. They provide strong constraints on the various models of the unification of three out of the four forces of nature (all except the gravitational).

A dream of the physicist is to prove that the fourth fundamental force of nature—the gravitational—is also linked with the others. In such endeavours, what the physicist is aiming at is to show the harmony of nature. The future of physics, says Salam, holds out many surprises. 'The more we seek to simplify, the more complicated it becomes,' notes the TIFR's former Director, Dr. Sreekantan, 'but man's search continues. It is in his nature to do so and unravel even a part of the mystery of the making and the working of the universe.'

In the field of cosmic ray studies, through Dr. Bhabha and, latterly, other scientists like Dr. Sreekantan, the TIFR has an unbroken record of studies right from its inception. In his original proposal to the Sir Dorabji Tata Trust, Dr. Bhabha had stated that the Institute would devote itself to the specific study of cosmic rays, for which the equatorial region is more suited than the higher and lower latitudes which are more affected by the magnetic pull of the poles. India has since maintained its early lead in the field. Dr. Bhabha conducted his experiments at the Institute of Science, Bangalore, and over the years the TIFR has developed, in a very major way, its own balloon facilities at Hyderabad. Here foreign scientists come to collaborate in experiments, flying instruments in balloons more than 100,000 feet high. Cosmic ray experiments have also been carried out at the Cosmic Ray Laboratory, Ooty, at an altitude of 7,000 feet. In this laboratory, cosmic rays are studied using a cloud chamber—the largest in the world — constructed by the TIFR a quarter of a century ago.

The Unreasonable Effectiveness of Mathematics

Mathematics, rightly viewed, possesses not only truth, but supreme beauty—a beauty cold and austere, like that of sculpture.

Bertrand Russell

Mathematics helps not only to explain or systematise facts already known but to discover fresh facts. Newton saw the apple fall, or so the story goes, and went to his desk and mathematically worked out his laws of gravitation and his explanation of the movements of the heavenly bodies. But Einstein did not function in quite the same way. He conducted no experiments himself and made no direct observations. He examined the mathematical consequences of Newton's laws and compared them with the findings of the experimentalists and he and others found that things did not always quite square with Newton's theories. So Einstein worked out mathematically a theory that would not only explain all that Newton did, and also much that Newton's laws could not explain. But he went further, on the basis of his theory. He said that certain phenomena would be observed under certain conditions—phenomena that had never previously been observed. Experimental observations proved Einstein correct. He had mathematically worked out the existence of certain facts before anyone had observed them. Nobel Laureate, Wigner, spoke of 'the unreasonable effectiveness of mathematics'; Einstein demonstrated it. Thus mathematics and 'fundamental research' go hand in hand and the vital need for a strong school of mathematics in the TIFR was something Dr. Bhabha aimed at from the very outset.

What was the state of mathematics in India 50 years ago when Dr. Bhabha first proposed to the Sir Dorabji Tata Trust that the Institute should devote itself primarily to mathematics and physics (especially cosmic ray studies). Professor M.S. Narasimhan writes that there were then:

only a very small number of good mathematicians in India, working in isolation in a few universities; there were hardly any experts in most of the domains which were in the mainstream of mathematics . . . .[1]

In one generation India made the leap and established herself in the forefront of mathematical research. There is a story behind it.

Dr. Bhabha was looking for a capable mathematician to start the school of mathematics at the Institute. He invited Professor K. Chandrasekharan who was working at that time at the Institute for Advanced Study, Princeton. The Professor accepted Bhabha's invitation and in the early 1950s they planned a programme to organise mathematical research. Students who had completed their master's degree were carefully selected and they were given in the first year an elementary but wide survey of many basic fields of mathematics so that they would never be too narrow in their thinking. In the second year they were introduced to more advanced topics by the staff and visiting mathematicians. In the 1950s, in several basic fields of mathematics, there were no experts in India and distinguished personalities from abroad were invited to give lectures and conduct seminars. The staff was also given good working conditions and was enabled to maintain continuous contacts with leading mathematicians abroad. Summer schools were organised periodically to which teachers from all over India were invited. The entire country received, we might say, a mathematical face-lift.

Today the TIFR, with its faculty of 70 mathematicians, is reputed to be one of the largest concentrations of its kind.

Among the French mathematicians who nursed the school in the early stages was Laurent Schwartz, winner of the Fields Medal in Mathematics. After his first visit in the fifties, he went to Paris and reported enthusiastically to his colleagues: 'I have met students at the Tata Institute who are the salt of

---

1 *Developing Mathematics in Third World Countries*, North Holland Publishing Company, 1979.

the earth!' In a letter to the Director of the Institute he wrote, in 1971, 'I consider that the Tata Institute is a remarkable achievement and is without parallel in any other country.' The USA, Japan, France, West Germany, Russia and the UK rank among the most advanced in the field of mathematics, and in that Big League is India.

To keep India's eminent position needs constant effort. TIFR's School of Mathematics like the School of Physics welcomes students at the M.Sc. level or equivalent to become Research Scholars with a stipend and hostel accommodation. There are usually 150 such scholars at a time. At the school level the Homi Bhabha Centre for Science Education promotes excellence in mathematics teaching in schools and colleges by working on curriculum and textbooks production, and competitions — the Maths Olympiads when foreign students are invited to compete with Indian ones.

Searching the Skies

'The technical devices which form the basis of the present economic and cultural strength of the Great Powers can be traced back . . . to fundamental scientific investigations which were carried out in the abstract, supported without thought of direct practical benefit,' says Sir Bernard Lovell, British Astronomer Royal. He points to the investigations of Faraday in electricity, Clerk Maxwell in electro-magnetic waves, and Lord Rutherford in atomic structure. 'Fundamental research,' he concludes, 'in astronomy or any other subject is an essential component in the welfare of modern civilisation.'

Astronomy is one of the oldest of sciences. Since time immemorial, man has searched the high heavens and tried to map the sky. Ancient India was particularly advanced in astronomy. Her clear tropical skies and her situation close to the equator provided plenty of scope for sky-searching. There are quite a few famous names in Indian astronomy led by that of Aryabhata.

The world's first optical telescope was built by Galileo in 1609 with a lens just 4 cm wide. Ever since, astronomers have been striving to make bigger ones. The refracting telescope uses lenses. The reflecting telescope uses mirrors and the largest ones are the 200-inch mirror telescope at Mt. Palomar, USA, and the Soviet 236-inch mirror telescope in the Caucasus. In making optical and radio telescopes, the scientists bow to the genius of nature. They find that the ability of a human eye aperture (of 1-mm diameter) to grasp visible light if translated into a radio telescope at a wavelength of one metre, will need an antenna four kilometres long!

In the 1930s, the radio was coming into prominence and scientists found that, in short-wave communication across the Atlantic, there were sources of radio interference from outside the earth. These were tracked down in 1931 by an American astronomer called Jansky with his backyard apparatus. The interference, it was confirmed, came from outer space. Radio waves are emitted by highly energy particles as they speed through the void with velocities close to that of light.

In his book, *A Window in the Sky*, A.T. Lawton says:[2]

> If the heavens of the optical astronomer are dusted with starlight then those of the radio astronomers are littered with noise. This 'noise' is created by naturally produced radio waves received via an aerial or antenna, amplified by a radio receiver, and then are made to operate a loudspeaker or—more likely—a pen recorder. Most of the noise sounds like the hiss of escaping steam or the roar of an aircraft jet exhaust at full power. Some special noises sound like ancient breathless steam engines while others are more like rusty hearth crickets.

The radio astronomer has learned to decode and read these noises and deduce certain properties associated with the objects producing them. His position is closely akin to the doctor who must diagnose heart, chest or lung complaints through the sounds they produce.

---

2 David and Charles, London, 1979.

In the early sixties, a group of young Indian astronomers training in the USA wrote three letters home, one each to the Council of Scientific and Industrial Research (CSIR), to the University Grants Commission (UGC) and to Dr. Homi Bhabha at the TIFR. They offered to come and work in India if they were given adequate facilities. Dr Bhabha promptly offered to provide facilities and invited them to return. The young team, led by Dr. Govind Swarup, decided to take advantage of India's location near the equator for observation

Radio Telescope

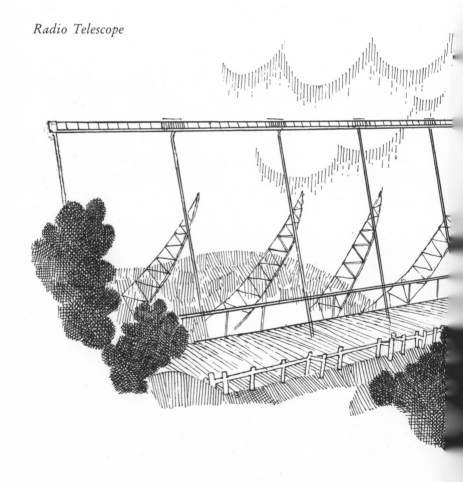

purposes. To this end they decided to design, fabricate and erect a radio telescope entirely with Indian know-how. The Tamil Nadu Government allocated a site for the telescope on a hillside in Ootacamund. Ooty is only eleven degrees north of the equator and the slope of the hill site is also eleven degrees. Tata Consulting Engineers helped in the structural and mechanical design and fabrication. In 1971 the telescope was commissioned.

Located near the geographical equator, the special feature of the design of the Ooty Radio Telescope provides for large

gathering power and also sufficient steerability at a relatively low cost. The instrument has a reflecting surface which is 530 m long and 30 m wide. Although operating on only one wavelength of about 1 m, the Ooty Radio Telescope is about three to four times more sensitive than the 250 ft. dish at Jodrell Bank in England. One of the unique features of the telescope is that its axis of rotation is parallel to the earth's axis of rotation. This was feasible only in India. The telescope beam is steered in east-west direction by mechanical rotation of the telescope and in north-south direction electronically.

As the Ooty telescope has a large effective area and a high sensitivity, radio sources almost at the fringe of our galaxy can be monitored by it. A pen-chart records the waves and whenever the moon intervenes, the pen-line drops sharply, to rise again when the object emerges from behind the moon. For analysis and interpretation the results are fed into a computer acquired with the help of a generous grant by the US National Science Foundation. The complex electronic system was built by a team headed by N.V.C. Sarma and M.N. Joshi. The location of the telescope in India enables it to explore both the northern and southern skies. The screening capacity of the telescope is widened by the addition of smaller satellite radio dish telescopes.

The Ooty telescope is at a par in its authority with the world's handful of great telescopes. Its findings are accepted by the other observatories and it sometimes undertakes joint programmes with them, as it did with the Sydney Observatory. In a joint programme, India and Australia discovered seven pulsars. So far, about 150 have been discovered in space. Pulsars are rapidly rotating collapsed stars which send out signals at perfectly regular intervals. In fact, they are fantastic clocks ticking away in space.

Of what use is this Ooty Radio Telescope to India? Astronomers at Ooty are engaged in the fundamental research involved in understanding the evolution of the universe. Pursuing this activity incidentally helps India to develop indigenously advanced electronic systems and computer processing of signals and images. With the experience gathered through designing and fabricating the Ooty Radio Telescope, the engineers of the TIFR, Tata Consulting Engineers, the Electronics Corporation of India and the Indian Space Research Organisation have designed and fabricated indigenously antennas.

Thanks to the Tata Institute of Fundamental Research, India has the know-how to set up the most powerful facility in the world for astronomical research in the metre and decimetre wave bands.

As a result of India's skilled scientists and geographical position, a Giant Metrewave Radio Telescope (GMRT) is being set up by the TIFR as a National Facility at Khodad, 80 kms north of Pune. The academic headquarters of the GMRT is located in the University of Pune Campus.

The GMRT has been designed to investigate a wide variety of celestial objects, ranging from our solar system to the very edge of the observable universe. An important scientific goal will be to verify the hypothesis of the Big-Bang Model for the origin of the universe. This Telescope will search for massive neutral hydrogen clouds which are expected to have existed some 15 billion years ago, prior to the formation of galaxies, according to the Big-Bang Model of the origin of the universe. The GMRT can study the epoch of galaxy formation.

When the Governing Council of the TIFR was discussing this project the scientists said they had the know-how but were daunted by the cost. J.R.D. Tata as Chairman encouraged them: 'Whatever the cost let us plan for the best facility of its kind in the world.' The Union Government had the vision to back it up. Not too far from this facility at Khodad, on the Pune University Campus, Dr. Jayant Narlikar, former Professor at the TIFR, has set up the Inter-University Centre for Astronomy and Astrophysics. Unlike in the West, where a lot of original research is done by the universities, in India university talent is wasted and research is concentrated in specific laboratories. This Centre enables university professors and research students to have access to the most modern — and well appointed — facilities for their creativity.

Astronomers at Ooty also have to reckon with the great issue of the origin of the universe and their conclusion supports the 'Big-Bang' theory. We on this earth live in the Milky Way galaxy. Astronomers estimate that there are billions of such galaxies, not just individual stars but entire galaxies, in the universe and the universe is expanding all the time.

Apart from being 'an essential component in the welfare of modern civilisation,' as Lovell has said, knowledge of astronomy may also have a part in the balanced development of man himself. Dr. John Matthai, at a reception given in his honour, recommended the study of astronomy. He said that if only we realised that the planet we lived on was nothing more than an overcrowded and slummy suburb on the outer fringe of a third-rate galaxy, we would perhaps not take ourselves so seriously.

Chapter 10

People and Projects

Ours is to be in many ways the job of pioneers building up science in a backward country, and though this may make it more difficult it also makes it more worthwhile and the achievement will be greater.

Dr. Homi Bhabha to astrophysicist,
Professor S. Chandrasekhar[1]

Between the high heavens above and the deep mines below that claim the TIFR's attention, lies the good earth. One person who walked upon it was an obscure glassblower in Bangalore, H.L.N. Murthy. For Rs. 1.50 a day he worked with his hand-bellows, shaping from imported glass tubes, intricate shapes for Sir C.V. Raman's laboratory. Later he established a wayside shop called The Mysore Scientific Glassblowers. Dr. Bhabha who had met him in Bangalore recognised his genius. As soon as the TIFR started he called Murthy to Bombay and suggested he wind up his wayside shop and join the TIFR in January 1946. Murthy was not only a glassblower but also a genius at fabricating precision equipment and one of the first things Murthy did in the TIFR was to make a Geiger-Müller counter. Dr. Bhabha sent him for a laboratory arts course to the Bristol University and arranged to pay his fees. After Murthy had arrived at Bristol, Dr. Bhabha got a message from the University that they needed no payment of fees or boarding charges to keep

---

1 This letter inviting the well-known astrophysicist in America to join him was written by Dr. Bhabha on April 20, 1944. Dr. Chandrasekhar was awarded the Nobel Prize in 1983.

Murthy. They found him so useful that they would like him to stay on as long as he could be spared.

From the Bristol University Dr. Bhabha sent Murthy to Metropolitan Vickers to learn precision mechanics. On his return to India, Murthy trained a large number of glassblowers and mechanics from the Atomic Energy Establishment, Bharat Electronics and the Indian Institutes of Technology, thus strengthening the laboratory workshop base of the foremost scientific institutes of India.

In 1960, Murthy (who had a congenital heart complaint) needed urgent medical attention. Dr. Bhabha arranged for him to be operated at the Boston General Hospital. Dr. Scanlon was informed that the patient coming to him was 'not just a glass technician, but an asset to India.' Dr. Scanlon cancelled his vacation and operated without charge. Dr. Bhabha had lined up eighteen blood donors for Murthy's open heart surgery. Murthy was kept in a good climate for recuperation. He was sent for training to the Corning Glass Works in America and to Philips in Eindhoven. He returned

Glass blower

to give thirteen valuable years to the Institute and another six years to his private business in Bangalore.

'Murthy,' Dr. Bhabha used to say, 'has the temper of a Spanish duke.' But that did not prevent the Institute from looking after him and building up through him, in many institutes of India, a corps of laboratory technicians, without whom scientific geniuses are often of little use today.

In 1965, Anand S. Panchal, a TIFR carpenter, was struck by a serious illness and was entered into the free ward of a public hospital. The next morning he was visited by Dr. Bhabha who removed him to a private nursing home with a night and a day nurse in attendance. 'He is not a carpenter but an artist,' said Dr. Bhabha of Panchal. Panchal died in 20 days. Murthy survived for 20 years. But the effort and the intensity of care devoted to each of them was at the same level. For the TIFR each person is precious.

In 1981 Dr. Das, who had gone to attend an international conference at Bonn, contracted galloping leukaemia. He died within ten days but the Institute and the Tata Trusts together ensured that his wife was rushed to his bedside in his last days.

Beyond the culture of science is a culture of care where people matter and not only projects.

Widening Horizons

At the TIFR, research is conducted over a wide spectrum. It ranges from research into the nervous system of the fruit-fly to studies on continental drifts. Considered in terms of electronics, the essential units in the brain of a fly and of a human being are based on similar systems—resistors and capacitors. Hence the interest of the molecular biology department in the study of the fruit-fly.

In 1925, geological evidence was advanced that 200 million years ago some parts of the world, including India, moved from near the South Pole to their present positions. The data collected and analysed by the TIFR provides strong support to this hypothesis of continental drift.

The TIFR was an early entrant into the field of computers. The first computers constructed in the mid-1950s were at IBM and some universities like Princeton in the USA. In 1954, when the computer science and technology section was set up at the TIFR, an instrument group set to work. None of the participants had any experience in using a computer, leave alone manufacturing one. Only one of the six, R. Narasimhan, had ever been abroad. The decision was taken to build a full-scale general-purpose digital computer and so it was built, ready for functioning by 1960, with characteristics comparable with one of the first computers manufactured at Princeton about the same time. Since then, computer technology has surged ahead in the hands of private companies, leaving academic institutions, who were among the pioneers of computer technology, far behind. In the 1960s, the TIFR not only used its original computer TIFRAC but also maintained and operated advanced imported computer systems. It made its facilities available to educational institutions, petroleum companies, space research, airlines and others. Because the TIFR came in on the ground floor of computer technology, it provided an institutional base and academic and professional know-how that it could share with the rest of the country. Students of the Indian Institutes of Technology come for advanced training to this national centre.

In 1973, the United Nations Development Programme decided that the TIFR was the best place in India to locate the National Centre for Software Development and Computer Techniques (NCST). NCST is now a separate institute independent of the TIFR. The computer programme grew around Professor R. Narasimhan. One of the major projects of the Centre is to design typewriter keyboards for various Indian scripts.

The TIFR's Basic Dental Research Unit has undertaken a major programme for studying the prevention of mouth cancer. It has made a detailed study of 1,50,000 persons in five States undertaking a laboratory examination of the lesions and has kept records with pictures. Follow-up studies of 66,000 individuals spanning twenty years have been completed. This study has shown that it is feasible to educate villagers to stop and reduce their tobacco chewing and smoking and this would have significant impact on the risk of oral cancer. Seldom has such a long-term study been undertaken in any part of the world. The findings from this study had an enormous impact in India as well as all over the world. This study has been done with the financial backing of the National Institute of Health, U.S.A.

A Fountainhead

What is so remarkable about the TIFR is not only the fact that it was given inspiring leadership during the lifetime of Dr. Bhabha but that those he trained have carried on his tradition and have given added momentum to the work that he started. Professor M.G.K. Menon, F.R.S., came to the TIFR as Reader in Physics in 1955. He was closely associated with Dr. Bhabha and was trained by him. Eleven years later, he succeeded Dr. Bhabha as Director. It was Professor Menon who pressed forward with developments in electronics and computer science, so that today the TIFR has become a supplier of know-how for India's defence and space programme requirements. The strength of the TIFR in areas of practical application has grown considerably since Dr. Bhabha's time.

'Professor M.G.K. Menon not only maintained and furthered with distinction the high level of research activity of the Institute but was also largely responsible for the increased involvement and commitments of the Institute in the nationally relevant applied areas of research and development, particularly in the field of electronics and computer science.' This is the assessment of the TIFR's third

Director, Dr. B.V. Sreekantan*. Professor Menon went to the Government of India as Secretary, Department of Electronics, became Secretary to the Ministry of Science and Technology, a member of the Planning Commission and Minister for Science and Technology.

Dr. B.V. Sreekantan is a cosmic ray expert. He has a gift for making complex scientific matters simple enough for the layman to understand. He ranks the TIFR, in its quality of research and in the range of its endeavours, as 'one of the premier research institutes in the world.' The Institute has 600 associate staff, Ph.D. students and—unusual for India— only 5 peons, to serve its miles and miles of corridors.

Dr. Sreekantan observes that the Institute's most important contribution to India is in supplying scientific manpower at the highest level, a role which till the 1950's was fulfilled mainly by Bangalore's Indian Institute of Science created through the vision and financial support of Jamsetji Tata. Dr. Sreekantan says: 'Our experience shows that if you train people in fundamental sciences, they can man any technological project or assignment. Our people have shown it in the field of atomic energy, of electronics and the space programme.'

Professor Yash Pal, a former student and a faculty member of the TIFR, became the first Director of the Space Applications Centre at Ahmedabad. Later he became Chairman of the University Grants Commission. Another student and faculty member, Professor Devindra Lal, became Director of the Physical Research Laboratory, also at Ahmedabad.

Dr. Sreekantan speaks of the multiplier effect of the TIFR on India's scientific skills. For its cosmic ray research, the TIFR perfected the manufacture of balloons at its Hyderabad Centre. Today, the balloon facilities are available for India's communication system and defence needs. Designing and

---

* Director till 1987, he was INSA Ramanujam Professor at the TIFR till 1992.

fabricating the radio telescope at Ooty gave India the know-how on antennas that has helped her to construct, entirely with indigenous know-how, the Satellite Communication Station at Arvi, and later other earth-stations. Microwave techniques developed at the Institute assist the defence services in the manufacture of critically needed transreceiver cells. Now a separate unit for microwave techniques is to be established in New Bombay.

The early mastery gained by the TIFR in manufacturing electronic equipment for atomic uses came in useful when its scientists went to the Atomic Energy Establishment. Later, the field developed so fast that a separate Electronics Corporation of India was founded as an off-shoot of the TIFR, manned by experts who were once with this Institute.

The phenomenal growth of the TIFR has been made possible by the financial support of the Atomic Energy Commission which today meets its budget of approximately Rs. 50 crores. The Trust's financial contribution now is peripheral.

What part, then, does the Dorabji Tata Trust play in the present set-up. 'Its distinctive role,' says Dr. Sreekantan, 'is in the part it has played and continues to play in the shaping of the Institute through the Council of Management.' Since the inception of the Institute the Chairman of the Council has been a representative of the Trust, a position occupied for the last three decades by J.R.D. Tata. Another person who was intimately associated with the shaping of the Institute from its inception in 1945 till 1980 was Professor R.D. Choksi. It is he, as mentioned earlier, who supported Dr. Bhabha from the very start and helped in the formulation of the shape and the policies of the Institute from the time it had a staff of six. TIFR's former Director Prof. Sreekantan assesses Tatas major contribution as 'the time, attention, experience and wisdom' that Professor Choksi has brought to bear on all major decisions over 35 years. Jamshed Bhabha, brother of the founder of the TIFR became chairman of the TIFR in 1994.

No Ivory Tower

Lights burn at the TIFR till late into the night and facilities are available at all hours of the day and night for those who are pressing forward with their research—and it is surprising how many do continue after office hours. But the TIFR is far more than one of India's prestigious research centre. It is the harbinger of a new culture. Dr. Bhabha's standing orders on cleanliness and standards of maintenance have already been quoted. Dr. Bhabha set the tradition that canteen tables should never be cluttered with uncleared plates and till today every customer in the canteen clears his own plates and dishes. Dr. Bhabha also wanted a canteen where the high and the low dined together. As Professor R. Narasimhan observes, the TIFR has 'instituted certain practices that break down vertical walls between people. We have still managed to retain this distinct culture which basically goes against the culture of the rest of the nation. As you can imagine it has not been easy but it has been possible.'

One often thinks of scientists as people who live in ivory towers. This is a temptation to many at the TIFR but quite a few delight in venturing out, lecturing, writing and even working occasionally outside the Institute. Be it on elementary particles, space exploration, the solar eclipse or genetic engineering, the TIFR scientists are educating the nation. In 1968, two of them were wondering what to do to improve science education in India. One of the first major programmes that emerged from their concern was the development of new curricular material for standards V, VI and VII based on a guided discovery approach, including kits and apparatus and textbooks. They tested it in ten schools of the Bombay Municipal Corporation, following up with regular visits to the schools and fortnightly meetings with the teachers.

When this programme was young, the scientists approached the Government of India for assistance but there was little response and so they approached the Sir Dorabji Tata Trust. The Trust sanctioned Rs. 15 lakhs over a five-year period, and so the Homi Bhabha Centre for Science Education came into being. Professor B.M. Udgaonkar recalls that he went to Professor R.D. Choksi one day with a few colleagues for what he thought would be a general discussion of the educational programmes at the TIFR and came back with the promise of support for the creation of the Homi Bhabha Centre for Science Education. 'A sensitive Trust can take a quick decision where official bodies may find it difficult,' said a TIFR official.

Professor V.G. Kulkarni of the TIFR left his work in the main campus and took charge of the project which now operated from a new municipal school building until it shifted to its own premises at Chembur on the outskirts of Mumbai. The Trust support was continued at a slightly lower key for a second period of five years. And so the TIFR has helped pollinate the field of scientific education in India. Scientific know-how, given the right setting and people, moves on its own momentum.

Professor B.M. Udgaonkar, who started research as a student of Homi Bhabha and has internationally recognised research in elementary particle physics, is one of the scientists who has stepped out of the ivory tower and tries to relate science to the needs of people. Besides being instrumental in the creation of the Homi Bhabha Centre for Science Education, he has influenced many reforms and new programmes at the University of Bombay and later, through his membership of the University Grants Commission, in the larger university system in the country.

Over the last three decades many of the finest scientific minds of the developing countries have settled down for higher research in America and Europe. As World War II was coming to an end, Dr. Bhabha had the same chance. At the age of 31, he had been elected a Fellow of the Royal Society, the second youngest to have been so elected. At the end of the War he had the choice to pursue his own research. Professor Maurice Pryce, later Wykeham Professor of Physics at Oxford, invited him back to England, saying,

'I think it would be very good for English theoretical physics if you would return to England.' Bhabha declined. He had decided to devote himself wholeheartedly to the scientific advancement of his own country, then on the threshold of Independence. As he wrote to Professor B.M. Udgaonkar later in 1963, 'For every thousand scientists who can do reasonably good work in a good scientific atmosphere, there is only one who can create the atmosphere for himself in a place where it does not exist, and this alone is a test of the outstanding scientist.' Many others followed in Bhabha's footsteps and spurned foreign offers. In so doing they have not only put their country on the scientific map of the world but have provided a model to scientists of their own and other developing lands.

The Multiplier Effect

The waters of the Arabian Sea lap the shores of Mumbai's Southern shores. Lush trees, and a well-trimmed lawn, lead to the impressive building of the Tata Institute of Fundamental Research. On a winter morning birds from colder climates twitter among the bushes and the trees, rejoicing in the quiet of the place. On a rock hardby in the sea a white *egret* with its tall legs stands in solitary grandeur. As one enters the main building the bust of the Founder, Dr. Homi Bhabha, greets the visitor. Another bust at the Institute is that of Dr. Albert Einstein by Epstein, and a third of Ramanujam, the mathematical genius.

The walls of the Institute are adorned by paintings of the finest Indian artists most of them selected in the 1950s and 1960s by Dr. Homi Bhabha. Among the many painters are Ara, Bendre, Hussain, Hebbar and Sabavala. It is one of the finest collections of modern Indian paintings. In these unusual surroundings Indian scientists work to unravel the secrets of nature.

Since Dr. Bhabha's untimely death three decades ago, 'the Institute has enlarged but the spirit remains the same', says

Dr. S.K. Mitra. Dr. Bhabha left behind the legacy of professional standards which are recalled today. Dr. Mitra says Dr. Bhabha was scrupulously honest in all the scientific work he did. He had no juniors to assist him in his personal research. When the burden of administration was too great, he sent round a circular to say that as he would not be able to do research, he would not be called 'professor' but will be addressed as 'Dr. Bhabha'.

*   *   *

The evidence for the interaction of cosmic rays was measured at TIFR for the first time. The first evidence for the interaction of cosmic neutrinos with matter was obtained in deep underground experiments at the Kolar Gold Fields. Charged states of cosmic-ray heavy ions were accurately measured by the Anuradha experiment which was flown aboard NASA's space shuttle "Challenger".

TIFR scientists were the first to demonstrate the effectiveness of Beryllium-10 as a 'clock' for the dating of rocks in ocean beds. A Carbon-14 dating laboratory was set up to determine the age of archaeological samples.

Scientists at the Institute have been successful in identifying a new class of superconductors (borocarbides), and have studied the nature of magnetism in various exotic substances.

Novel optoelectronic devices have been designed and laser techniques have been used to fabricate superconducting thin films.

The electronics group of the TIFR was the nucleus from which the Electronics Division of BARC grew. Eventually it led to the establishment of the Electronics Corporation of India (ECIL) at Hyderabad.

Over the years a number of TIFR scientists moved elsewhere in the country to lead a host of departments, laboratories and institutes. Several others have served on national policy-making bodies.

*   *   *

Extremely high energy collisions between particles help us grapple with the question 'What is matter made of?' What elementary particles exist, how can they be classified, and what is the logic followed by Nature?

Accelerators of the required energies are extremely expensive to build, and the two largest in the world are located at the European Organization for Nuclear Research (CERN) in Geneva, and at the Fermi National Laboratory (Fermilab) near Chicago.

While our domestic consumer electricity power is 220 volts, this accelerator, known as Pelletron can produce power up to 14 million volts to create high energy collision of particles which scientists can study. Prof. S.K. Mitra requested his colleague to switch off the Pelletron and took the author into the bowels of the tall Tower explaining various facets. While his learned explanations were proceeding, the author was impatient to finish the tour at the soonest lest somebody, by oversight, switched on the electric power!

TIFR scientists are engaged in major ongoing collaborations at both CERN and Fermilab accelerator laboratories, and some sections of the particle detectors used at these sites are designed and fabricated here. The Institute has recently contributed to the important discovery of the 'top' quark at Fermilab, and to the study of the properties of the 'Z-boson' at CERN.

An exciting project on which progress has been made is that of talking to computers. Can we make them recognise our speech? Can we teach them to answer back? TIFR scientists have been working on these problems: speech recognition, script recognition and speech synthesis. These involve the study of natural language, grammatical patterns, and so on. Computer scientists at TIFR have also been involved in developing defence and communication systems.

The TIFR's Multiplier Effect has influenced the growth of science in India.

*   *   *

At its Golden Jubilee Celebration in January 1996, TIFR's Director Virendra Singh,* an eminent physicist, summed up TIFR's philosophy of growth perhaps relevant for other institutes:

1. One builds up groups and laboratories around outstanding men, and not the other way around.
2. Work has come first, buildings afterwards.
3. Choice of areas of work is given great attention for their potential for significant developments as well as our own strengths.
4. Philosophy of self reliance has been emphasised right from the beginning.
5. One has depended on creating one's own qualified manpower without having to deplete other Indian institutions.

*   *   *

Though mainly occupied in fundamental research, the TIFR has a lot of human talent with potential for applied and technological research yet to be tapped. This application of fundamental research of the Institute to practical applications in technology will prove a fruitful next step.

---

* So varied are the activities of the TIFR that some of them have hardly been touched upon in these chapters. They are the fields of Theoretical Physics, Nuclear and Solid State Physics, X-ray and Gamma Ray Astronomy, Chemical Physics and Molecular Biology. Those interested in knowing more about these are requested to refer to Appendix 'K' where there is a summing-up of the TIFR's work over the last 50 years by its Director, Dr. Virendra Singh, on the occasion of its Golden Jubilee Celebrations.

A sketch of the Nobel Laureate physicist Prof. P.M.S. Blackett by Dr. Homi Bhabha

Part V

NATIONAL CENTRE

FOR

THE PERFORMING ARTS

Chapter 11

An Idea is Born

The House of Tata spearheaded India's modernisation in science and technology. In the same house was born a project to help in the revival and preservation of India's ancient heritage in music, dance and other performing arts.

In 1966, Jamshed Bhabha (Homi's brother), a Tata Director and Trustee of the Sir Dorabji Tata Trust, proposed to his fellow Trustees the idea of a National Centre for the Performing Arts. He envisaged something more than an Indian equivalent of the Kennedy Center in the USA. He felt it should be the endeavour of the institution 'to maintain the continuity of the great teachers of Indian music, dance and drama and to record and preserve the finest performances in these arts.'

Jamshed Bhabha was convinced that, to meet India's needs, any centre for the performing arts would have to be different from such centres established in the affluent countries of the West, such as the Lincoln Center in New York or the Kennedy Center in Washington or the South Bank Complex of theatres in London. The Indian centre would, he believed, have to be much more than a well-designed and beautiful venue for the performance of music, dance or drama. It would have to be concerned equally with systematic archival recording of the arts in urban centres and rural areas, and with the continued maintenance of the traditional master-pupil links through well organised 'Master Classes'. He stressed that, since the music of India does not have a form of notation and cannot be represented on paper like Western music, the art has been handed down and kept alive for centuries by the guru personally passing on his art and knowledge to his pupils, frequently his own children or other members of his family. With growing industrialisation and new job opportunities in the cities, this old relationship between the guru and his pupils is fast disappearing. If public institutions did not take action to save India's heritage of music, dance and drama, it may be lost to mankind forever, just as the musical heritage of ancient Greece was lost for want of recording. At the same time, with modern techniques it should be possible to devise an adequate system of notation for Indian music also.

Many of the Trustees initially viewed the proposal with scepticism. J.R.D. Tata and Professor Choksi (then Managing Trustee) supported it, because, as Mr. Tata said, 'while we want to build a prosperous society, we do not want to be merely a materialistic consumer society.' After an animated discussion, the Trustees gave Bhabha the green light, conditional on his finding a suitable site large enough for the centre that he dreamt of. Some Trustees thought that to obtain 5 acres of land in Bombay was so formidable a task that the scheme would never get on the ground, let alone off the ground.

The Trust's appeal for a plot for the projected institute of music, dance and drama was submitted to the Maharashtra Government. Its first response was to offer an extensive area near the Ellora Caves! To match this highly original suggestion, Jamshed Bhabha asked the Government of Maharashtra for permission to reclaim an area of five acres off Marine Drive opposite the Taraporevala Aquarium. The Government acceded to this novel request, subject to clearance from the departments concerned, including the Central Water and Power Research Station at Pune. The latter objected to any reclamation by the traditional method of a bund or sea-wall with earth filling, as any such reclaimed area would deflect the sea-currents and cause erosion of the adjacent sands of Chowpatty beach. It stipulated that the entire area of five acres should stand as a concrete platform on stilts above the sea. This posed an insuperable problem. To build such a large platform would by itself have cost two or three crores of rupees, at a time when the only funds on the horizon for the new project were the Rs. 50 lakhs*

---

* Rs. 5.9 crores of 1997. Another Rs. 20 lakhs were ploughed in by 1983.

earmarked for it by the Dorabji Tata Trust as a sponsoring grant.

However, Government's agreement in principle to the reclamation of an area off Marine Drive for the project represented a major breakthrough as far as getting a plot of land in Bombay was concerned. Availing of it, Bhabha then sought the permission of the Government of Maharashtra to reclaim a similar area at the end of Marine Drive, beyond where the Oberoi Hotel was to come up. The Government agreed. The Trust's entire sponsoring grant of Rs. 40 lakhs literally went into the Arabian Sea but it gave the Centre its first five acres and later three more acres of prime land which is today as expensive as real estate in New York. The lease rent—Re. 1 per year for 99 years.

While the reclamation was in progress, a fund collection drive was launched with the support of J.R.D. Tata. This was the first public project sponsored by the Sir Dorabji Tata Trust for which wide financial support was sought from other forward-looking trusts, organisations and individuals. The size of the funds required for its realisation made this necessary. The rupee had its value and money was not as plentiful in the sixties as in the nineties.

An initial hurdle was the hesitation of many persons in a position to help who thought that the arts were only of peripheral importance for a developing country like India. What this philistine view overlooked was that, in India, music accompanies us from the cradle to the grave and is an inseparable part of the canvas of our lives. Perhaps more than any other country in the world, India's arts are closely integrated with religious and spiritual values, and some of its greatest music and forms of dancing are related to worship and originated in the temples.

The first three grants came from the Sir Ness Wadia Foundation, the Mafatlal Foundation and the Mahindra Foundation, followed by the Godrej Foundation and from the V.D. Chowgule organisation, and a handsome personal donation from Jehangir Nicholson. The Dorabji Tata Trust joined by Ratan Tata Trust sanctioned an additional grant. A host of Tata Companies pitched in most generously, taking the Tata total to Rs. 2 crores out of the aggregate sum of Rs. 3 crores collected till the Tata Theatre came up in 1980.[1] UNESCO contributed high fidelity recording equipment and the Ford Foundation provided, through a grant of $ 200,000, the foreign exchange required to cover specialised architectural and acoustic consultancy services from abroad. The funds collected from non-Tata sources aggregated well over a crore of rupees including donations in kind, such as the gifts by Sir Dinshaw Petit (III Bart.) in memory of his wife, Lady Sylla Petit (sister of J.R.D. Tata) of the beautiful Italian Carrara marble staircase of Petit Hall, four lustrous Waterford chandeliers (for the Tata Theatre), and an exquisite Louis XVI Sèvres cabinet to adorn the Little Theatre of the National Centre.

As soon as this institution had been registered as a public trust, Jamshed Bhabha, as the Trustee-in-Charge of the project, proceeded to set up for it a Board of Advisers, consisting not only of men and women from India with an outstanding record of service to the performing arts, such as Ravi Shankar, Satyajit Ray, Vilayat Khan, M.S. Subbulakshmi and Zubin Mehta, but also distinguished friends of India abroad with personal experience of performing art centres, such as Yehudi Menuhin, the Earl of Harewood, Jean-Louis Barrault, Gian-Carlo Menotti, Dillon Ripley, Karl Bohm and Andre Malraux, the then Minister of Culture in the French Government.

Yehudi Menuhin was enthusiastic about the plans to preserve the arts of India which have become 'an inspiration to the whole world'. Mrinalini Sarabhai spoke of the 'enormity of the task you have set before you' to meet the 'desperate need' for such a central institute. Renowned conductor, Bombay born Zubin Mehta, was thrilled that his city was at

---

1 Rs. 3 crores of the period is equivalent of Rs. 11.5 crores of 1997. Major contributors: Tata Steel, Indian Hotels, Telco, Tata Chemicals, Tata Oil Mills, Voltas, Tata Electric Companies and the Indian Tube Company.

last pioneering the 'preservation of the performing arts' and was planning to make available facilities as good as anywhere in the world. Dr. Narayana Menon, eminent musicologist, became the first Executive Director of the National Centre for the Performing Arts (NCPA) as the centre was named. Dr. Menon had been released from his post of Director-General, All India Radio, with the consent of the Prime Minister, Mrs. Indira Gandhi, to enable him to take up the appointment.[2]

The Kennedy Center took 14 years to complete, with all the resources of the United States and land readily available beside the Potomac river. Building India's National Centre could have been expected to take much longer since the land had to be reclaimed from the sea. While this was being done, the National Centre started its activities in the premises offered to it on Bhulabhai Desai Road by Mrs. Madhuri Desai, Chairman of the Bhulabhai and Dhirajlal Desai Memorial Trust. It was here that the National Centre's programme of work was inaugurated in January 1969 by Mrs. Indira Gandhi. 'I think it is inspired by great vision,' she said, 'and I sincerely hope that it will be sustained by a sense of dedication.'

Though conceived as a National Centre, the sponsors wanted the culture of all lands to breeze through it. An international division was planned to cover the music, dance and performing arts of other regions of the world and stimulate cross-fertilisation of ideas.

Even before the Tata Theatre or the teaching and research block were constructed, the Centre spearheaded in India the observance of Beethoven's two hundredth birth anniversary with the public release in Bombay of a commemorative postage stamp and with a festival of some of Beethoven's famous works performed by Yehudi Menuhin, Louis Kentner and the Cologne Trio.

To record the musical heritage of India in far away villages and small towns, a special air-conditioned and acoustically treated van was built to house the high-fidelity mobile

---

2 Dr. Menon relinquished the post of Executive Director, NCPA in December 1982.

recording equipment donated by the John D. Rockefeller III Foundation. There are places where a van cannot reach and it requires a jeep to go into the remote rural areas and bring the village artistes to the van for recording. The total collection of audio and video recordings in the archives of the NCPA is 4293 hours which includes 320 hours of folk music recordings in the States of Rajasthan, Gujarat, Maharashtra, West Bengal, Kerala, Uttar Pradesh and Madhya Pradesh.

As can be imagined, this national endeavour is a highly time-consuming and an expensive one. Before these journeys take place, it is advisable to work with a local authority on folk songs who knows where the artistes are located in the remote villages. While recording in Rajasthan, the National Centre was fortunate in having the guidance of an authority on Rajasthan folk songs, Komal Kothari,

National Centre for the Performing Arts

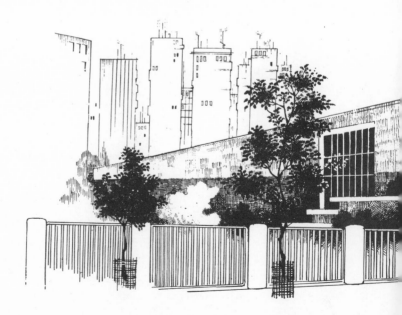

who runs an institute of his own. Kothari directed the van to where the artistes live in the villages. Only three States have been covered so far. States which have a good road network, like Tamil Nadu and Kerala, could quickly have their folk songs recorded by the NCPA provided certain facilities are made available.

The task of recording the folk music of India, according to Dr. Narayana Menon, is almost as great as that of the Geological Survey of India in trying to locate our minerals. It can go on for ages, but with each passing day some heritage, somewhere in India, may be lost. The constraints of finance and staff are very major handicaps. After the songs are recorded, an index is made giving details of the dialect of the area, the script of the translation and other particulars, which can be of great interest to research scholars.

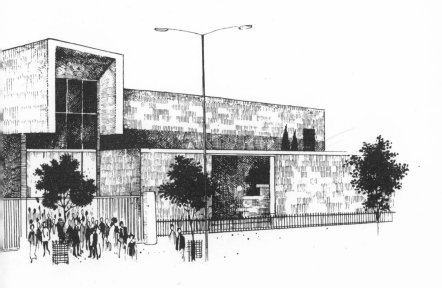

While field activities were under way, in Bombay, the site was reclaimed and the first building, the training and research block, was erected. 'Master classes' were held by *gurus,* such as the distinguished *tabla* player of Hindustani music, the late Ustad Ahmedjan Thirakwa; the renowned *sarangi* player, Pandit Ram Narayan; and the equally well-known *surbahar* teacher, Annapurna Ravi Shankar, the Kathak and Odissi dance maestros, Mohanrao Kalyanpurkar and Kelucharan Mahapatra.

For indoor recording at the Centre, it was decided not to have an impersonal studio with glass windows and green and red lights as in most radio stations, but to build a recording auditorium which could accommodate about a hundred. Many an Indian artiste likes his disciples to sit around him and he gets a fillip from appreciative admirers stimulating him to greater heights with their nods and *wah-wahs.* The 114-seat recording auditorium gives enough scope for a select public audience too. It also serves as a small multi-purpose theatre for performances of music, dance and drama, as well as for the screening of great films of the past.

A library of books, records and tapes has been created. The music library has facilities for lovers of music to sit and listen undisturbed to their favourite compositions. There are already air-conditioned facilities for preserving on tapes and films, the masterpieces of Indian music and of the Indian screen.

The research block has a project to analyse components of the design and construction of Indian musical instruments which currently vary greatly in quality because of a lack of standardisation and quality control in manufacture. The keynote instrument of Indian music, the one that gives the sustaining note, is the *tanpura* which is made from a gourd, a natural product. Miraj in Maharashtra is a centre for its fabrication by traditional artisans. When a young NCPA representative went to explore how they could help, the local artisans were deeply suspicious and feared that big business was manoeuvring to take over their ancestral craft.

They supplied the young man with wrong information to begin with but slowly he gained their confidence and the true facts emerged. Today, the computer is a tool which has become an inherent feature in every other modern work-place. Significance of application of computer-techniques in the field of music is that it reveals the mysteries of music. It is only due to the sophisticated and advance tools of analysis that we are able to have a microscopic view of the physical aspects of music. A computer-assisted analysis of North Indian classical music (vocal and *bansuri*) has been carried out with a view to understand some of the aspects like pitch, intonation, melodic movement, effect of the textual element in vocal music, etc. For want of appropriate tools, these problems had hitherto remained elusive to empirical scrutiny. The results of this study suggest that the computer technology can be successfully deployed towards furthering our understanding of music. However, the challenge of developing the necessary software to match the 'mindware' of musicians must be met with.

Foyer of the Tata Theatre

Chapter 12

Cathedral of Sound

Waves of the Arabian Sea stirred by the monsoon fury lash at the retaining walls of Marine Drive, Bombay. The rhythmic regularity of the waves sounds like a movement from nature's monsoon symphony. A hundred yards from the sea stands the Tata Theatre. As the waves beat outside, within the sound proof walls of the Theatre a Ravi Shankar could be playing the sitar.

The Tata Theatre was conceived not as just another concert hall but as one linked to the National Centre, to perform a distinctive cultural service. For seven years the finest acoustic and architectural consultants in the world wrought to erect this Cathedral of Sound. After careful scrutiny, Philip Johnson of the US, one of the architects of the State Theatre of the Lincoln Center for the Performing Arts, was chosen as the architect.

In 1972, when Jamshed Bhabha was in New York, Philip Johnson recommended a Danish acoustic consultant who had worked in collaboration with him at the Lincoln Center. Subsequently Bhabha visited the Kennedy Center for a performance of 'The Swan Lake'. He was shown round the auditoria of the Kennedy Center by Dr. Dillon Ripley, Head of the Smithsonian Institution, and a Member of the National Centre's Advisory Board. Bhabha was enthralled by the quality of the acoustics which he thought were superior to that of any of the auditoriums of the Lincoln Center or of the South Bank Complex of theatres in London. He decided that evening that the acoustic consultant of the Kennedy Center was the one India needed. It turned out to be a soft-spoken Professor of Electrical Engineering and Architecture at Columbia University, Professor Cyril M. Harris.

Harris was a man with a dry sense of humour and firm opinions of his own. Earlier, Philip Johnson had worked with Harris on the eastern wing of the Museum of Modern Art, New York, and Johnson recalled that 'the personal chemistry (between him and Harris) had been less than perfect.' So when Bhabha came back to Philip Johnson in New York and said he wanted Harris, Johnson was not exactly enthusiastic. However, he did pick up the phone and, to his surprise, got an extremely warm response from Harris. Johnson gasped with surprise and whispered, 'I think he must have got wind of the National Centre project and wants to be in on it.' *The New Yorker* was to write later (November 8, 1976):

> Harris had been thrust upon Johnson, and that fact alone might have caused some ruffling of feathers, for ordinarily on an auditorium job the architect retains an acoustic consultant . . . and thus the architect is the consultant's boss. In the case of the Bombay concert hall, Johnson got the commission and was told soon afterwards by his client, Jamshed Bhabha, that the acoustic consultant was to be Cyril Harris . . . Johnson was dismayed.

The New Yorker adds that Johnson still wanted the Bombay assignment because it was a real challenge, and in next to no time, Johnson realised to his pleasure that Harris, though stubborn about acoustics, admired Johnson for being stubborn about aesthetics. 'The better the architect, the harder the acoustic consultant has to work, and that is as it should be,' Harris said.

The New Yorker reports how, working for the Tata Theatre in Bombay, Cyril Harris and Philip Johnson began to appreciate each other to an extent that made Johnson remark: 'We have got along well because Cyril understands everything I say about architecture and I do not understand a word of what he says about acoustics.' Both of them drew funds only for their bare expenses. They charged no professional fees. They did it as their contribution to the arts of India. At the India end, Johnson was assisted by Rustom Patell and Harris by Burjor Mistry. Johnson and Harris not only had to find compatibility with each other, they also had to give attention to the request of their clients—the Chairman, J.R.D.

Tata, and Jamshed Bhabha, both of whom looked into details of the construction.

Although it looks one piece, the Tata Theatre is built on two distinct rock structures and has two different foundations. As one enters the lobby from Marine Drive, one hardly notices within a few yards a black line on the floor. This consists of mastic, a type of oily cement, placed between the two buildings to absorb vibrations and ensure that road drilling or other disturbances on the front on Marine Drive do not disturb the peace of the auditorium.

Most theatres have a rectangular foyer. The Tata Theatre has one grand foyer stretching for 300 feet from one end to the other. Soon after one enters it, there is a little garden on the right. The architect wanted to build a high wall beyond the garden to shut out the hawkers and the cars on the main road. Mr. Tata and Mr. Bhabha suggested that it might be kept open so that the visitors to the theatre could absorb the beautiful view of Bombay's skyline. Johnson replied: 'Allow me to build the wall, but I will give you a picture window.' He did; and through the window is now visible a wonderful panorama of the city framed in the brown grey stone of the building.

In the theatre's upper foyer, the Indian engineers wanted to have a column at a point of intersection of the beams. But the column would have intruded into the view of the sea and Malabar Hill, so Johnson, perfectionist as he is, refused to agree to the construction of a column, and, instead, got the engineers to instal, at the point of intersection of the beams, a specially designed stainless steel screw. The screw is only six inches in diameter and six feet long held by a nut at the roof level. The screw, which bears a tremendous load of concrete, had to undergo X-Ray tests to ensure its strength and safety before being placed in position, but it did serve Johnson's purpose of providing a beautiful vista of Bombay clear of any column.

During his three visits to the city prior to starting the design of the theatre, Johnson noticed the traditional practice in India of the audience sitting around the performers in a semi-circle, and this must have given him the idea of designing India's first national theatre in a fan shape with a steep rake for unobstructed clarity of view from every row and every position in the auditorium. By having a theatre of this shape, instead of the traditional 'horse-shoe' or 'shoe-box', he was able to ensure that no member of the audience was further away than fifty-five feet from the performers on the stage. The theatre is divided into five equal segments making a 1040-seat theatre.

As requested, Philip Johnson and Cyril Harris designed this auditorium for performances without recourse to electronic amplification. One of the major challenges was to ensure an even distribution of the sound. This is not easy to achieve in modern architecture with its plain wall surfaces. One of the principal reasons why the opera houses and theatres of the 19th and earlier centuries were generally superior to those of modern design is that they had a great deal of surface decoration in the form of cherubs, garlands, mermaids and other design devices on the walls, balconies and ceilings, in addition, of course, to the chandeliers. All these embellishments served the possibly unintended purpose of breaking up and distributing the sound evenly over the whole auditorium. In contrast to this, the plain flat or curved surfaces of modern architecture cause the sound to bounce off into focal points, making some parts of a modern auditorium good and others less satisfactory or even bad. It is for these reasons that many people found an old auditorium like the Carnegie Hall superior to the newer Philharmonic Hall in New York.

To take the place of the embellishments of earlier centuries, Johnson and Harris used a unique acoustic device in the shape of tetrahedral forms, hand-made on the ground in reinforced plaster, alternately convex and concave, and raised into position individually in the ceiling. Much later Harris admitted that only the skilled low-cost labour of India made it possible to use this device successfully, and that such a theatre could not have been constructed in America for love or money. Later, at the renovated Philharmonic Hall in New York, Harris and Johnson used a similar device, but one that, in the rectangular form of that theatre, did not entail skilled labour for variations in the shape and size such as had been required for the fanshaped theatre in Bombay.

Harris was keen that even the sound of air-conditioning should not disturb the quality of music. He said that it should be such that even if he sat alone in the auditorium, he should not hear the air being blown in. 'The cool air should drop down noiselessly,' he said. To meet this requirement, air ducts of a much larger size than normal were installed and a proportionately larger air-conditioning plant installed.

As the stage had no proscenium or curtain for a change of sets, Mr. Tata and Mr. Bhabha proposed having a rotatable stage of a light material like aluminium. Harris said that aluminium would 'drum' the sound. He wanted a rotatable stage of reinforced concrete six inches thick. And so it was built as heavy as a railway turn-table. The steel framework of the turn-table had to be constructed in the works of the Tata Iron and Steel Company at Jamshedpur and transported in segments by road in giant trailers over the distance of a thousand miles. It is a marvel to watch how this massive stage turns almost noiselessly and comes to a stop within a hairline of the main stage wall.

No expense was spared to make this theatre the pride of India. Soon after the opening of the Tata Theatre in October 1980, the National Centre for the Performing Arts got requests when a foreign dignitary be it a Prince Charles or a Margaret Thatcher was visiting India, to put on a suitable programme for them at the Theatre. In the early years of this century when the Taj Mahal Hotel was built, Jamsetji Tata had hoped that visitors would come to this city because it had a superb hotel. Today, visiting dignitaries and lovers of the theatre fly to Bombay just for an evening at the Tata Theatre.

*   *   *

Echoes of the Arts

Round the centre piece of the Cathedral of Sound are the echoes of the arts. The NCPA's master plan envisaged by Jamshed Bhabha had as part of the NCPA complex a theatre for experimentation and drama. In 1982, on the Platinum Jubilee of The Tata Iron and Steel Company, its Chairman, who was also Chairman of the NCPA, J.R.D. Tata, announced a generous grant from the Company for a 300-seat Experimental Theatre: 'I am very happy that this old Company born out of the inspiration and pioneering spirit of Jamsetji Tata, shows 75 years later, that it is still open to new pioneering ideas.'

The theatre was formally inaugurated four years later by Russi Mody, as Chairman and Managing Director then of Tata Steel, who remarked that Bombay was fortunate to have such a facility and the Company regarded itself privileged to be associated with a project which would contribute greatly to the cultural enrichment of Bombay.

In the Experimental Theatre, the stage and the seating on its 3,300 sq.ft. floor area are not fixed but made up of modules which make possible a variety of arrangements. The 33-foot high ceiling has a grid-frame and cat-walks to provide total flexibility for lighting and prop facilities. Its surrounding high balconies for audiences can also be used for performances in special dramas such as 'Romeo and Juliet'. The theatre with its excellent acoustics is also frequently used for chamber music and solo recitals on the piano. For the rising generation of playwrights, actors, producers, directors and musicians, the Experimental Theatre gives scope for innovation and creativity.

Further developments at the NCPA were born out of the offers to it of grants from many sources. The first was the Ford Foundation's grant of seventy-five thousand US dollars coupled with a presentation of a beautiful collection of old photographs by an American friend of India, Judith Mara Gutman, which resulted in the establishment of a Centre for

Photography as an Art Form (CPA). Jehangir Nicholson, a distinguished collector of modern Indian art, made a donation to set up a Museum of Modern Art to which he would lend a part of his extensive collection of modern Indian art for exhibition and storage. A valuable area on the first floor of the Teaching and Research Block was allotted to what is called the Jehangir Nicholson Gallery of Modern Art, which, apart from featuring examples of modern Indian art stored by the NCPA, is also being used regularly for valuable and important exhibitions of paintings, sculptures, ceramic ware, prints and in other forms of the plastic arts. A subsequent donation for this project by Dilip Piramal resulted in the CPA having its present Art Gallery referred to as the Piramal Gallery. Both the Nicholson Gallery and Piramal Gallery are greatly in demand throughout the year for representative exhibitions from within India as well as exhibitions sponsored from abroad by cultural agencies, such as the USIS, the British Council and the Max Mueller Bhavan.

A Dance Theatre

To meet the need of a compact Auditorium (smaller to, but a little larger than, the Little Theatre, which is heavily booked throughout the year), a Theatre of two hundred seats was designed and built to permit an easy dialogue between the performers on the stage and members of the audience. A generous donation from the Godrej family in memory of Soonabai Pirojsha Godrej, brought into being what is now called the Godrej Dance Academy Theatre. Inaugurated by the head of the Godrej Organisation, Sohrab P. Godrej, this Auditorium successfully meets a need of the NCPA which cannot be so well fulfilled by its larger Auditoria. A neat garden is set before the Godrej Dance Academy Theatre.

The NCPA has also set up within its framework three new collaborative departments engaged in valuable innovative activity. The first, based on an initial donation from Shaila and Jagdish Parikh and continuing monetary and organisational support is the Mohile-Parikh Centre for the Visual Arts (MPCVA). This was followed on a similar basis by the Jindal Arts Creative Interaction Centre (JACIC) under Sangita Jindal as its Honorary Director, and the Morarka Centre for Research and Revival of Crafts (MORCRAFTS) with Sangita Kathiwada as its Honorary Director. Under the over-all leadership of Vijaya Mehta, NCPA's Executive Director and Trustee, all three units have made valuable contribution to the cultural life of Bombay.

*   *   *

MARG Publications

Over half a century ago when high quality colour printing was not so common the first issue of MARG came out. It was an illustrated magazine dedicated to presenting the classical and contemporary arts of Asia and, in particular, of India. It carried authoritative commentaries from scholars supported by beautiful pictures and old prints. It covered such themes as:

The Golden Age: Gupta Art, Empire and Influence;

Odissi — Indian Classical Dance Art;

The Jewels of India.

MARG, printed at the Tata Press, also covered historic places like Goa and Bombay with rare pictures and sketches. For nearly four decades its distinguished editor was Dr. Mulk Raj Anand.

As one might expect, such a magazine produced on high class art paper made losses for decade after decade. It was kept going by the conviction of J.R.D. Tata that a corporate house needs to support what the country needs and it was his vision that the glory of the arts of India should be presented to the country and the world.

MARG was supported by Tata Sons for many years, but when Tata Sons ceased to be a private limited company and other investors took shares in it, Mr. Tata took steps which ultimately resulted in this creative activity to be passed on to the National Centre for the Performing Arts. The conviction of Mr. Tata was translated into reality by the zeal of many, especially of Roshan Sharokh Sabavala and her dedicated staff. Today, Mrs. Sabavala is no more but her work is carried on by her daughter, Radhika, and others.

*   *   *

Drama and Opera House

By far the largest of the NCPA projects is the drama and opera house complex under construction as we go to press. It owes its origin to two people who appreciated the Tata Theatre, J.R.D. Tata and Indira Gandhi. J.R.D. Tata said what he missed most in the Tata Theatre was a classical proscenium with a stage-curtain. The quality of the sound and the sight-lines of the Tata Theatre are admirably suited for performances of Indian music, dance and drama. By a coincidence Indira Gandhi as Prime Minister of India, attended the gala performance of Rossini's 'Barber of Seville' in the Tata Theatre. The seats of one of the five blocks had to be pulled out to accommodate the 60-member orchestra. She remarked to Jamshed Bhabha that it was a pity that the theatre did not have an orchestra-pit. She mentioned to him the need for a National Centre to have a theatre with a proscenium with a stage-curtain and an orchestra-pit. Sadly, that was her last engagement in Bombay before her tragic assassination on her return to New Delhi.

*   *   *

On the shores of the Arabian Sea at Nepean Sea Road stood the magnificent mansion of Sir Dinshaw Petit, Baronet. Almost a century ago, as the mansion was under construction, Italian workmen were singing *O Sole Mio* and *La Donna e Mobile*, as they were setting up a Carrara marble staircase from Italy.

Every stone was numbered and set up according to the plan from Italy.

Many decades later, Jamshed Bhabha took with him the renowned Californian Architect, Welton Becket, to Petit Hall just before it was torn down to make way for a smaller and more practical building for the family. Welton Becket was the architect of the Music Centre in Los Angeles. Zubin Mehta had strongly recommended him to Jamshed Bhabha to be the NCPA's architect, long before the Tata Theatre or any of its smaller buildings had been constructed. It was Welton Becket who, at the meeting with Sir Dinshaw Petit, remarked with enthusiasm how beautiful the Chandeliers of Petit Hall and its unique baroque Carrara marble staircase would look against the austere background of a modern Auditorium. Sad to say, Welton Becket, who had offered his services to the NCPA free-of-charge, died on his return to America.

Shortly after his departure from India, Sir Dinshaw Petit, the Third Baronet, who had listened in silence to Welton Becket's remarks, invited Jamshed Bhabha for a drink and silently handed to him an official letter addressed to him by Prof. Rustum Choksi, then Vice-Chairman of the Indian Hotels Company, offering to purchase for the Taj Mahal Hotel, the Petit Hall's Chandeliers at a lakh per chandelier. Jamshed Bhabha, as his cousin, both being descendants of the first baronet Sir Dinshaw Petit, addressing him by his familiar first name, said "Fali, it is a very good offer and frankly if you are in need of money, you should accept it." It was only then that Sir Dinshaw announced for the first time that he had already decided to present to the NCPA Petit Hall's Chandeliers and the Carrara marble staircase in memory of his wife Sylla (the elder sister of J.R.D. Tata) who had died of cancer. With the utmost care, piece by piece, the entire staircase was dismantled, and stored for almost two decades. When the drama and opera house came up in the mid-1990s, every piece of marble was polished and reassembled again with precision. With its beautiful supporting columns and its graceful curves, the staircase of incredible beauty leads the visitor to the first floor of the opera house. There is probably nothing like it in the finest palaces of India.

This private benefaction is being put to public use just as the four grand chandeliers of Petit hall adorn the Tata Theatre. Wealth shared is joy multiplied.

Designed originally for a 2000-seat theatre, similar to the Opera House of the Kennedy Center for the Performing Arts in Washington, the new Auditorium has an exceptionally large stage with a high loft for flying scenery and a very wide proscenium opening, approximately the size of the Covent Garden Royal Opera House before its present renovation. Unfortunately, however, an unexpected and deplorable reduction of the Floor Space Index (F.S.I.) made it unavoidable to reduce the seating area from 2,000 to about 1,300. While its acoustics, as already tested are excellent, the new Theatre has one welcome feature lacking in some of the great and otherwise beautiful auditoria of the West, namely, that every seat commands an unobstructed view of the whole stage. The Theatre, relatively small though it be, will be one that Bombay (now Mumbai), can be legitimately proud of.

In 1994 when the Drama Opera Theatre and the Arts Complex was still on the drawing boards the Deputy Chairman of the NCPA, S.A. Sabavala, proposed that independent of the celebration of a particular birth date, the Drama Opera Theatre and related Arts Complex should bear the name of Jamshed J. Bhabha, who originally conceived the National Centre for the Performing Arts and with determination and dedication piloted its growth and development to its recognised stature as a Centre of National Importance. The proposal was warmly seconded by P.L. Deshpande and N.A. Soonawala and adopted unanimously by the Council of the NCPA.

Part VI

OTHER VENTURES

Chapter 13

National Institute of Advanced Studies, Bangalore

Ideas have the strange habit of cropping up even decades after they are first mooted. J.R.D. Tata's mother was French and, on his occasional visits to France, he was intrigued to learn that 70 per cent of the top jobs in the Civil Service, the scientific institutions and even the banks of France were occupied by men who were trained at one of the four *Grande L'Ecole Polytechniques* of France. The first of these Polytechniques was started by Napoleon with the very practical purpose of training civil engineers he required in the course of his campaigns. France, unlike some other countries, pays great attention to education and next to the Prime Minister's position the most important Cabinet rank is held by the Minister for Education. The syllabus of these *Grande L'Ecole Polytechniques* has been refined over the years to produce some of the finest practical intellects of France.

In the 1960s, J.R.D. Tata wondered whether there was room to start a similar institution in India. Thorough as usual, he wanted an expert report on the state of Indian education and whether there was need for an institution like that. He invited Professor Jean Capelle, Director-General of Education, France, to go round India with a group of educationists from within the country to report whether a similar institution would be beneficial to India. Mr. Tata wanted to submit such a proposal to the Nehru Memorial Trust for which he had already raised a substantial sum of money. The Nehru Memorial Trust was thinking at that time of erecting statues of the former Prime Minister and investing in some other minor ventures.

J.R.D. Tata placed this Capelle Committee report before the Nehru Memorial Trust. The Chairperson was Indira Gandhi, who had been elected Prime Minister some months earlier. The former Maharaja of Kashmir, Dr. Karan Singh, was the Secretary. One important condition for those who were admitted to a *Grande L'Ecole Polytechnique* is that all the participants had to be good at mathematics because mastery of mathematics is believed to be an aid to clear disciplined thinking and decision-making. Dr. Karan Singh, a philosopher, found this insistence on mathematics objectionable. 'Do you mean to say,' he asked Mr. Tata, 'that if I am not good at mathematics I cannot join the proposed Institute?' Mr. Tata replied that he could not and explained why. Indira Gandhi turned up her nose at this and said, 'Jeh, the Institute is elitist.' J.R.D. Tata was disheartened.

Looking back he said, 'Perhaps I should have pressed ahead and got Tatas to undertake this project.' Meanwhile, J.J. Bhabha had proposed a National Centre for the Performing Arts and J.R.D. Tata enthusiastically supported it. The Trust having already institutions of social science, medicine and fundamental research in science, an institution of the arts was the next logical step.

Although he did not take up the *Grande L'Ecole Polytechnique* project, the idea of starting a suitable Institute of higher learning for India abided with him. In 1984 when he decided to shed the chairmanship of Tata Steel, which had occupied a great deal of his attention, Mr. Tata went back to his original idea. Times had changed. The educational scenario of the mid-1980s was very different from that of the 1960s. When J.R.D. Tata first thought of the equivalent of the *Grande L'Ecole Polytechnique*, the Indian Institutes of Management were about to start and five Indian Institutes of Technology had just started. By the 1980s the major Indian Institutes of Management and the IITs had established themselves as outstanding institutes of higher learning.

On a visit to France in 1984, J.R.D. Tata invited Professor P. Olmer, former Director-General of Higher Education, Ministry of Education in France, to form another Working Group and assess the sort of institution India needed in the 1980s. J.R.D. Tata selected for the Working Group the former

Director of the TIFR, Prof. M.G.K. Menon; space scientist, Prof. Satish Dhawan; civil servant, Mr. L.K. Jha; former Chairman of the Atomic Energy Commission, Mr. H.N. Sethna; and Trustee of the Sir Dorabji Tata Trust, Prof. Rustum Choksi. The Working Group members recommended an Institute of Continuing Education. They did so because the fund of knowledge is reported to double every seven years and no academic institute can prepare a person for a thirty-year career. The committee recommended an institute that would have a wider range of study though a much shorter duration than the IITs and IIMs. Those who would attend it would be those who had some years of experience in business, industry, education, the civil services and the like who had shown promise of leadership. The report spoke of the need for 'an institution that went beyond the IITs and the IIMs'.

It was in pursuance of this vision and the recommendation of distinguished men that the Sir Dorabji Tata Trust launched the National Institute of Advanced Studies (NIAS). Tata Steel, Telco and Tata Chemicals followed with generous grants.

Dr. Raja Ramanna who had stepped down as Chairman of the Atomic Energy Commission was appointed to head the Institute in Bangalore. The grounds of the Indian Institute of Science in Bangalore were selected as the site, for when Jamsetji Tata conceived of the Indian Institute of Science he wanted it not only to teach advanced science but to blossom into teaching humanities balancing the scientific temper with the richness of a liberal education.

At the same time that the Olmer Committee was formulating its report, there was the Platinum Jubilee celebration of the Indian Institute of Science, Bangalore. Mr. J.R.D. Tata who was President of the Court of that institution had his proposed institute very much in mind when at these celebrations in December 1984 he enquired whether the time had not come 'to review one of the original ideas Jamsetji had when he formulated his scheme for the Institute, namely, the inclusion, in some form, of some of the subjects usually referred to as the "Humanities". Jamsetji, when mulling over his scheme for the Institute, thought of education not only as a means of raising the standard of living of his countrymen but also their quality of life.'

He was obviously thinking of an Institute to complement the Indian Institute of Science. The new buildings of the National Institute of Advanced Studies were inaugurated on the Campus of the Indian Institute of Science by J.R.D. Tata in 1991, to provide this balance of the humanities and social awareness to those engaged in science, education, industry and the civil service.

The Institute has so far conducted eleven annual residential and participatory courses for senior executives from the Government at the level of Joint Secretary as well as promising executives from private sectors showing leadership qualities in their mid-career. This short course covers a wide spectrum of lectures, seminars, workshops, etc. on subjects as varied as history, philosophy, consciousness studies, problems related to women, international and strategic studies and epigraphy, etc. Each lecture is by an authority on the subject with enough time for the participants to interact with the speakers and amongst themselves.

Similar courses suitably modified are also being organised for senior lecturers and junior professors of the universities with special attention to women, the North-Eastern areas, Jammu and Kashmir and other isolated universities.

NIAS functions as a 'think-tank' covering a wide range of issues. The subjects dealt with by NIAS are those which are on the border-line of science, social science and the humanities. The research works taken up at the Institute are in the fields of knowledge which, hopefully, will have an impact on the problems of the country. It is also determined by the specialists available on the subject.

At present, it has Units for Health and Human Behaviour, Philosophy of Science including Consciousness Studies, Women's Policy Research and Advocacy, Environment, Epigraphy and International and Strategic Studies.

On the occasion of the inauguration of its J.R.D. Tata

Memorial Auditorium by the then Prime Minister, Deve Gowda, NIAS Director, Dr. Raja Ramanna, noted the salient points of the Institute.

'Besides doing high quality research in complex fields, which could benefit by the overlapping of one with the other, we also took into account the fact that we were in Karnataka and, therefore, we had to do something connected with Karnataka. It is for this purpose the Institute created a cell on Women's Policy Research and Advocacy (WOPRA) to collect and analyse data from actual field studies. A report has already been produced which will be in a programme for the amelioration of some of the badly treated sectors of humanity. We have had the support of eminent professors such as Prof. M.N. Srinivas, who is an eminent sociologist and an expert on caste; and Prof. B.V. Sreekantan, who was formerly the Director of the Tata Institute of Fundamental Research, Mumbai, and well known for his study on Cosmic Rays. Under the unit of Philosophy of Science, he and his collaborators have been working on the subject of Consciousness, and I have been pursuing a new approach to Nuclear Physics. One of the important studies, which has an overall impact on our development, is the study of Psychology and we have a Health and Human Behaviour Unit headed by Prof. R.L. Kapur, who has been investigating the causes of violence and the atmosphere needed for creativity among scientists. Prof. C.V. Sundaram, who was the Director of the Indira Gandhi Centre for Atomic Research, is with us looking into the Energy and Educational problems of the country. It will become too long to enumerate all our activities and I shall only name them. We have a unit on Environment for studying the reduction of the effect of insecticide and pesticide poisoning effects in soil and water. This is being done in association with the Indian Institute of Science. We have a unit on Epigraphy to assist archaeologists in their work by the use of computers and is supported by the Indian Space Research Organisation. We also have an important group on the study of nuclear problems involving nuclear armaments, nuclear testing and allied political issues. There is also a small unit on music to understand its physical and aesthetic structure with special emphasis on Purandara Dasa's works.

'It is not our intention to become a large institution even the 50, that we are, seems sufficient. However, the institution is based on the principle that, if we can find leaders capable of contributing in a creative way to developing new fields of knowledge, we will be happy to initiate and encourage that activity.'

Chapter 14

Vistas for the Blind

Under the shadow of the Sahayadri range, Western Maharashtra, a playful child picked up a hand grenade left by the soldiers during World War II. Minutes later the grenade exploded, multiple wounds scarring the tender face. Overnight Raghoo's world became one of darkness. As the years went by, he withdrew more and more into himself. Feroze Moos, who was a member of the staff of the Tata Agricultural and Rural Training Centre for the Blind at Phansa, relates his first meeting with Raghoo many years later:

> One had to crawl in to where he sat in the gloom. The smoke from the fire smarted in my eyes. I called him by his name but there was no response. His uncle said that Raghoo had stopped speaking a long time ago. 'Does he never move out of this place?' I asked, 'Sometimes, when he must relieve himself. At all other times, food and water are brought to him.'
>
> Raghoo was told to get up and come out of the hut. He did so without a word.
>
> It was very difficult to convince the family members to release Raghoo to come and train. The family confabulated. The emaciated blind man sat silently. I interrupted saying, I would like to ask Raghoo whether he would come with me.
>
> 'How can he tell you, he never speaks.'
>
> 'He is not dumb,' I replied.
>
> Turning to Raghoo I held him by the arm and gently asked him whether he would accompany me, told him that I would treat him like a brother, and give him the fruits of his toil. I called him by his name telling my name, who I was, where I lived and how I earned my bread. He remained silent, so I waited. After a minute or two had elapsed I again turned to him saying:
>
> 'These people tell me you are dumb. You are not dumb, Raghoo. Tell them so. Tell them you will come with me and return to teach them things of which they cannot learn.'
>
> The scarred face moved slightly and the lips opened. The boy indistinctly murmured. 'I will go with you and show them.'

He came to Phansa. The vistas he opened up to my mind were formidable. Abject darkness. How does one break the chalice of ignorance and pour from it the liquid which has enervated the soul for decades? For two months Raghoo refused to speak. He was slow of mind and his health was delicate. Sometimes he would stand for hours in one place till his shadow shortened and lengthened into an infinity. Who could help this man?

It took two years. He spoke, debated, laughed and sang as well as any other. What a vigorous farmer he was! Raghoo knew all the seasons. He tilled the earth with dexterity, built his own stable and lived his life with a certainty.

Raghoo was one of the more fortunate. It is estimated that there are about 9 million blind in India today, 90 per cent of them in the rural areas. Most of them are left in a corner like Raghoo or used to do repetitive work like drawing water from a well. Thirty years ago, there were 70 industrial homes for the blind in the urban areas but not a single one in rural India. In 1954, the first World Assembly on the Welfare of the Blind in Paris passed a resolution calling for training of the blind rural population. Uganda and Kenya were among the first to undertake this training. In 1959, John Wilson, Secretary-General of the Royal Commonwealth Society for the Blind, visited Bombay and found Shantilal H. Shah, the then State Minister for Law and Labour, keenly interested in the welfare of the rural blind.

The Dorabji Tata Trust was requested by the National Association for the Blind to be one of the contributors for the purchase of a farm at Phansa in Gujarat. As the Association failed to get the expected support from the Union and State Governments in time, it appealed to the Trust to underwrite the entire cost of the 245-acre farm. The Trust responded. Coconuts, chickoo and mango trees abounded by the hundred, but a lot of the land lay fallow, and before long, under the leadership of Captain H.J.M. Desai of the NAB, and the enthusiastic dedication of a young man called Feroze Moos, the first beginnings were made. When the first group of eight rural blind passed out, Prime Minister Nehru himself came to award the certificates and spent three hours at the farm.

How do you teach a blind man to till a field?

A string with pegs tied in at regular intervals along its length, is lined up. As he feels for the pegs, the blind man knows where to plant. Each blind man has a small plot of land which is his to plant, to water, and to cultivate. There is a demonstration plot with 16 crops which he can feel and learn to identify the plants. The speed with which a blind man can identify a crop can shame many a sighted person.

In these idyllic surroundings 60 of the rural blind are taught to look after a farm, after cattle, to weave with cane or sisal, to cook their own food, to wash their own clothes.

The first battle to be waged is against apathy. As one watches 60 students of the farm at Phansa water the plants, sing *bhajans,* weave cane, one is humbled. One's mind reaches out to those millions across the land who have no such opportunity to have the broken pieces of their lives put together.

The task of resettlement is as major as that of training. The resettlement officer has to find a suitable plot of land near the home base of the pupil and then equip a blind diploma holder with either cattle or water facilities. The idea is to integrate him with the sighted society.

In the growth of this Centre, the Governments of India and of Gujarat have each played an important part. The US Government has, over a period of time, given Rs. 5 lakhs. The Royal Commonwealth Society provided the first instructor and still continues aid for specific projects. The American Foundation for Overseas Blind has also helped. Since this Centre started, two similar institutions have been established in the South and in West Bengal. India has 9 million blind of whom 2 million are children. Every district of India should have at least one such institute.

Chapter 15

J.R.D. Tata Centre
for Ecotechnology

I believe that the social responsibilities of our industrial enterprises should now extend, even beyond serving people, to the environment. This need is now fairly well recognised but there is still considerable scope for most industrial ventures to extend their support not only to human beings but also to the land, to the forests, to the waters and to the creatures that inhabit them. I hope that such need will be increasingly recognised by all industries and their managements because of the neglect from which they have suffered for so long and the physical damage that the growth of industry has inflicted, and still inflicts, on them.

J.R.D. Tata
December 1969

Unlike other major institutions covered in this book the J.R.D. Tata Centre for Ecotechnology was not founded by the Trust but substantial support was extended by the Sir Dorabji Tata Trust to make it possible.

Thirty years ago Dr. Norman Borlaug succeeded in developing a hybrid seed that would multiply the yield of wheat many times over. India, which had just suffered from serious food shortages during 1964-66 necessitating the import of ten million tonnes of wheat largely under the US PL-480 programme, had two men of vision who decided to give India food security by taking this miracle seed to farmers into every nook and corner of India. They were the Food and Agriculture Minister, C. Subramanian, and the agricultural scientist, Dr. M.S. Swaminathan. With the political will of the Minister and the scientific and organisational capability of Dr. M.S. Swaminathan, a revolution in farming took place.

The wheat production rose dramatically to over 60 million tonnes by 1994, ten times the production of pre-Independent India. Meanwhile, our population spiralled from 300 million in 1947 to over 900 million in 1997. It is too dreadful to contemplate the catastrophic consequences on human lives and on environment if the yield of land has not shot up so dramatically. The impact on environment would have been disastrous, as people desperate for food would be clearing all forests and national parks with consequences to the flora and wildlife of India. But there is no room for complacency. As Dr. Swaminathan says, 'the Green Revolution has given the world a thirty-year breathing spell in terms of achieving a balance between population and food supply. This period, from 1970 to the end of the century, has allowed the international community to make adjustments in technologies, demographic transitions and natural resources conservation to compensate for population increases.' The question is 'What is the world and especially India going to do with this "breathing spell"?'

The Rio Conference on environment where heads of 170 nations participated was an indication that nations are awakening to the threat to environment from pollution, pesticides, earth-warming, indiscriminate use of limited resources which, coupled with a population explosion, growing joblessness, especially in the developing world is creating prospects of social and political tensions which could have great consequences. UNESCO, under the leadership of its Director-General, Dr. Fedrico Mayor, Commandant Cousteau in France and Dr. M.S. Swaminathan took on the cause of Ecotechnology in a systematic way.

The term *eco* was coined to describe environment friendly, socially and economically sustainable technology which combines frontier technologies with traditional wisdom of the tribals and the rural communities. The origin of the word lies in the Greek word *oikos* = home + *techne* = a craft of beauty. If technology is part of the problem it has also the potential to provide sustainable solution to negative features of contemporary development provided it becomes rooted in the principles of ecology, equity and ethics, in addition to those of economics. Such a paradigm shift in the strategies and policies relating to technology development and dissemination will lead to the growth and spread of a self-replicating ecotechnology movement.

Hitherto economics, sociology, technology and ecology were distinct disciplines. But to save the environment all four have to get together. As Dr. Swaminathan says: 'Development cannot be stopped. The question is how can we have sustainable development that is "pro-nature, pro-poor and pro-women".'

These words reflect the desire of the late J.R.D. Tata who was not only concerned with the environment (as quoted above) but was even concerned at — and never accepted — the poverty of our people as their unchanging fate.

Furthermore, nearly 11 million new livelihoods have to be created in our country every year. Most of these can only come from agricultural and rural small scale enterprises. In this scenario the sunrise enterprises are horticulture, aquaculture, production of hybrid seeds, processing medicinal plants and growing food suitable for the food processing industry. Dr. Swaminathan says that as economic development is bound to come, our job is to see that it is compatible with environmental and social alertness. Our traditional systems have much to contribute in this sustainable development when modern technology is married to it.

It is not enough if we oppose development; it is even more important to propose sustainable options for producing more food, income and jobs from diminishing per capita arable land and irrigation water resources. So when the proposal of Dr. Swaminathan to start a Centre for research and propagation of ecotechnology in Chennai (formerly Madras) came before the Trustees of Sir Dorabji Tata Trust in 1995, they sanctioned the required grant of Rs.1.85 crores (about half a million US dollars) for its initial years of working. In addition, some other Tata Trusts underwrote the cost of construction in Chennai (Madras), of Rs. 1 crore.

On the occasion of the first Asian Regional Workshop on Ecotechnology, Dr. Swaminathan announced that the Director-General of UNESCO, Dr. Federico Mayor, had given a further grant of US dollars 200,000 to the M.S. Swaminathan Research Foundation as an endowment to help further the goals of the Asian Ecotechnology Network for which the J.R.D. Tata Centre for Ecotechnology will be the nodal agency.

The UNESCO Director-General, Dr. Mayor, said: 'Tomorrow our children and grandchildren will inherit exactly what we have left them.' He proposed to the UN General Assembly of 1996 a declaration of the rights of future generations and responsibilities of the present generation towards succeeding ones.

The UNESCO chief thinks that the application of ecotechnology at different levels opens up 'immense opportunities .... for eco jobs related to saving the environment'.

How will the Ecotechnology Centres in Asia go about their task? The programme includes:

Providing training to the new generation of decision makers, be they in Government or industry or education.

Resolving the problems of soil erosion, salination of the earth, both of which could trigger off large-scale famines in future. Encouragement and popularisation at the field level of bio pesticides, bio fertilisers in preference to chemical fertilisers, vermiculture and other soil enhancing techniques. And demonstrating all this through pilot projects. (This work has already begun in the Pondicherry area).

Eco-forestry.

Eco-aquaculture (inlands and coastal).

Recycling of wastes.

Exploitation of solar, wind, biogas and biomass and their integrated use through models the governments could propagate.

Monitoring and control of air, water and soil pollution.

Promotion of a green health movement based on medicinal plants and organic foods. (At the field level the MSSRF has already worked in Tamil Nadu and Kerala.)

*   *   *

The Sir Dorabji Tata Trust's interest in environment had also led it to launch on a programme to save medicinal plants in the State of Maharashtra.

There are over 600 species of medicinal plants in Maharashtra, many in the Ghats. Many are exploited but not replenished. Others are destroyed by the custom of setting fire to field and mountain sides. India is estimated to lose 600 species of its plants each year. Any of these could have life saving properties and be lost to us forever.

The Trust has sanctioned a grant to an NGO for selected conservation areas in forests in co-operation with the Chief Conservator of Forests in Maharashtra and in a captive nursery at Karjat.

*   *   *

J.R.D. Tata Ecotechnology Centre has a strong database and a programme of dissemination. The Ecotechnology Centre is part of the Trust's wider concern for the environment.

A Trust has two roles to play. One is to deal with the immediate problem. The other is to look ahead. At a Trustees meeting it was observed that the big crisis facing India in the 21st century would be water. Soon after the World Bank in a report said that the wars of the 21st century would be over water. There is already conflict within India between States on sharing river water. Integrated harvesting of water in select drought water prone areas could be models for the future. A substantial grant was sanctioned for projects of watershed development.

Chapter 16

Rural Thrust

The road from Satara in Maharashtra going east to Maan Taluka is hardly frequented by cars. Some glorious old banyan trees line the road. Their drooping overground roots resemble the wispy beard of a Ho Chi Minh. The further you go the drier it gets and there are vast tracts of barren land where nothing grows. This is the area which the *Gazetteer of Bombay Presidency* (Vol. XIX) termed 'barren and desolate, sparsely wooded even near the river .... The ordinary sources of water supply are wretchedly precarious even for drinking .... The rains consist chiefly of periodical thunderstorms with intervals of incessant wind and dust tempered with an occasional drizzle.... The area of black soil is small and owing to the scanty rain and want of water works, what black soil there is yields but little.... Maan is subject to constant droughts.' Forty years ago the local people had few sources of livelihood. Some of them took to criminal activities and were jailed by the British rulers.

At the heart of this area lies the village of Devapur, 55 miles away from Satara town, deep in the interior, getting barely ten inches of rain annually. Many years ago, during a drought and famine, the British, for relief work, had the local people construct a huge water tank. But the water, alas, was not for them. It was to supply the city of Sholapur. Beside this blue expanse of water sits 71-year-old Sadashiv Hari Baber who recalls, in a voice not too soft, the early years of struggle. He wears a spotless Gandhi cap, and his kindly face, with several front upper teeth missing, bears a quizzical twist.

'You know,' he says, 'in 1945-46 we did not even have a school teacher for our children. Once a stray visitor walked into the village and, when asked, he said he was a teacher. We grabbed him and said we would give him *bhakri* (a

thick *chappati*) but no salary. The impoverished teacher stayed.' Then one day a distinguished man with a flowing white beard walked in and said he would like to establish an institution to educate the children of the area. He was Bhaurao Patil, a man with little education himself but with a passion to bring education to the doorstep of the villagers. Bhaurao insisted that if the villagers wanted him to open a school they would have to transfer to the name of his society, land which would be used to construct a hostel. The villagers could not quite understand this concept of a hostel. But Sadashiv's family agreed to give the land overlooking the lake. Now, decades later, Sadashiv realises that Bhaurao insisted on the hostel because, as a social reformer, he was convinced that the only way to break the caste system was to have young children live together and eat together. Today there is hardly any caste barrier in the village, thanks to Bhaurao's work.

Bhaurao showed the area to Professor D.R. Gadgil, Director of the Gokhale Institute of Politics and Economics, Pune. It was Professor Gadgil who in turn suggested to Dr. John Matthai, Chairman of the Dorabji Tata Trust, that if the Trust wanted to go in for rural work, as Dr. John Matthai did, this was the most challenging area they could work in. In December 1951, some months after he resigned as Union Finance Minister, Dr. John Matthai, presiding at a convocation of the TISS, announced that the Dorabji Tata Trust whose activities had till then been confined to urban projects would now turn also to village reconstruction, 'which provided a new field for valuable pioneer service.' The efforts of the Trust would, he said, with the help of Professor D.R. Gadgil, 'lead to a movement of rural reconstruction based on organised self-help and capable of expansion in due course by its own momentum.'

Sadashiv recalls the day in the early 1950s when Dr. Matthai and Professor Choksi first came to their village. Devapur was then some miles off the nearest motor road and so the villagers prepared a festive bullock-cart to transport them over the last lap of their journey. 'Dr. Matthai asked us to tell him what we would like the Trust to do and they would send the men to assist us in our development.' Sadashiv and his villagers requested that the Trust take on not only their village but also eight neighbouring villages for development. The Trust accepted the challenge. It started a subsidiary called the Rural Welfare Board (RWB) to look after this particular experiment.[1] Five young men were appointed: an agricultural expert, a commerce graduate, an accountant, a graduate of the TISS and a cattle specialist. In overall charge of the RWB was N.D. Godbole (who was also Secretary of the Dorabji Tata Trust). Older villagers fondly remember the late Mr. Godbole. The efforts of these outsiders and the villagers have dotted this once barren and parched land with several patches of lush vegetation.

The first six years were 'a period of boundless enthusiasm' according to Mr. Y.S. Pandit,[2] a member of the Rural Welfare Board. 'We tried to do too many things at once,' says S.R. Suratwala, one of the five young pioneers. A graduate of the TISS, he recalls how in the first flush of youth they tackled tasks which, looking back, they are surprised they ever undertook. They had neither car nor jeep at their disposal and there was no bus service in the 64-square-mile area they worked in. They cycled from village to village. After a hard day's work in the merciless sun, they would take night classes in literacy.

But there was a method in their zeal. After an initial survey, the RWB decided that the first priority was to stop soil erosion. The rainfall was often as little as in the deserts of Rajasthan, but when the rains did come, such was the uneven lay of the land that floods would result, washing away what little topsoil there was. The first task was to construct contour bunds on the land. These not only prevented soil

---

1 Later, the RWB took up projects at Mulshi (Pune District) and at Mithapur (Amreli District, Gujarat).
2 'Evaluation of the Devapur Project, Report', 1976.

erosion but helped to raise the underground water level in the whole area.

As a next step sisal was grown on the bunds—though not too successfully. The goats seemed to have developed a taste for it! Within five years, 8,000 acres were secured with bunds and the Board persuaded the government to take up another 6,000 acres for bund building. This labour-intensive activity gave work to about 400 people and injected, through work, funds into the local economy. Today, forty years later the same method is suggested for the rapidly dwindling ground water level to rise. The intervening years were wasted by India and it has still to wake up to impending water famine.

In the five years 1955-59 the Rural Welfare Board gave each of the eight villages a drinking water well, a school, a medical dispensary and a common community centre. The schools and the dispensaries were transferred to the local authorities who now run them. Thanks to electricity, which came to the area through an RWB loan of Rs. 7 lakhs to the State Electricity Board, 200 of the 400 irrigation wells are fitted with electric pumps. Nationalised banks instead of the RWB, now give loans for wells and pumps. Till the Trust took the matter in hand, there was not a single drinking water well in the area. Hookworm was widely prevalent. Availability of clean drinking water has wiped out the disease. Easy access to water has also made daily baths and clean clothes not only possible but, increasingly, the norm.

Soon other agencies like the Food for Work Programme also began functioning in the area. Old wells were cleaned up; new ones were dug. The cropping pattern has changed. Sadashiv shifted from growing *jowar* and *bajri* to cotton and wheat. The RWB has helped to start a cooperative cotton ginning plant which services 32 neighbouring villages. Years later it shut down because the cropping pattern changed and cotton was not remunerative to grow.

The cattle breeding programme has won acclaim—and prizes. In those early years of rural development, many were crossing Indian breeds with exotic cattle like Jerseys. The RWB project concentrated on cross-breeding Indian cattle and evolved a new breed by crossing the local Khillar with Rajasthan's Tharparkar bull. The cross-breed yielded seven to ten litres of milk per day against the yield of one or two litres of the local cattle. The cattle breeding programme, which won all-India awards, was conducted by Dr. P. Persai, a J.N. Tata Scholar who studied in New Zealand.[3] Technically Persai cannot be faulted but his greatest strength is his love for the animals. He has developed a sensitivity towards them and their needs. At night he lives within earshot of the cowshed and from sounds emanating from the shed he knows when a cow is in pain or labour. He then wakes up the cowhand to administer to it. The Cattle Breeding Centre had to confront the problem of marketing the milk in this remote area. Dr. V.P. Patil, former Dairy Development Commissioner of Maharashtra, says that where farmers had never seen a hundred rupee note in their entire lives, today, thanks to this milk scheme, they can see such a note every week. In due course of time the milk collection work has been taken over by the local cooperative societies and the buildings of the Centre have been handed over to the Gram Panchayat to start a high school.

The poultry experiment began well and farmers took to it and soon supplied all the local needs. But once they started on a larger scale they again ran into the problem of marketing. Since then, poultry farming has lost some of its attractiveness as a subsidiary activity.

Maan Taluka is sheep country, as is Rajasthan and other low rainfall areas. The RWB introduced Merino rams. The breed improved but the progeny of the Merino-cross rams did not secure any significant gain over the indigenous variety, nor did their white wool make a perceptible difference in income. Undaunted, the Welfare Board worked at exploring the right market for the wool and finally got

---

3 He also received a grant for higher studies from the Sir Dorabji Tata Trust.

Raymond Woollen Mills to be the purchasers. The Research and Development Division of Raymonds along with the RWB, organised an artificial insemination camp to which shepherds brought 6,000 Deccani sheep. Raymonds left behind Australian Merino and Polwarth rams now placed in 15 flocks in five villages for natural mating.

As against the meagre yield of up to half a kilogramme of coarse black wool per sheep per shearing, the crossbred progeny (50 per cent Merino and 50 per cent Deccani) is expected to yield about two kilogrammes of good quality white wool per sheep per shearing. Simultaneously, the increased weight of the sheep would also give a higher mutton yield. Thus the income of the shepherd per animal is expected to more than double.

Between 1958-59 and 1971-72, Devapur's per capita income went up by 236 per cent and agricultural output by 270 per cent. 'Formerly,' says Sadashiv, 'I alone had a bicycle in the village. Now every house has a bicycle and most also have a transistor.' In the village of Pulkoti, when this writer visited it, the *sarpanch* was engaged in the energetic task of listening to a cricket commentary—India vs. England. What is of particular significance is that in Devapur one could notice no caste differences. There and in Pulkoti, the Welfare Board, along with the government, has undertaken a special programme of housing for Harijans which has given them elegant little cement homes, each an independent unit of about 440 sq. ft. with its kitchen and washroom.

A lot of the gains of the villages' development has been neutralised by the sharp increase in population to nearly three times what it was when the Trust began with the project three decades earlier. The Board officials now regret they were not quick enough to start family planning work right in the beginning. They undertook it vigorously only mid-way, after 1967. Some villages in the area like Jambulni, Pulkoti and Devapur have since achieved prize-winning performances in this field, yet neighbouring villages like Gangoti and Panwan where the Board is also at work, proved resistant to family planning because of the influence of conservative elements and a different caste structure. One is struck with the infinite variety of India and the challenges it presents when villages within a distance of three miles of one another are so different in their response to the same programme conducted by the same people offering the same incentives.

The Devapur Project—probably the first integrated rural scheme undertaken by an Indian private agency—is a textbook case of development. Students of rural work can learn from its successes and its failures. In view of the growing importance of rural work and as the guidelines to corporate institutions and NGOs who are sincerely endeavouring to work in this field, it may be appropriate and useful if the findings of a note surveying work for 30 years up to 1985-86 are recorded. The report was made by Mr. Y.S. Pandit who had worked with Dr. John Matthai in the Tata Department of Economics and Statistics and in addition had a considerable understanding of rural Maharashtra. He was assisted by Mr. Suratwala, who himself played a significant part in the work at Devapur. The report says that there are two aspects of development:

1. To increase productivity and income; and
2. To improve their quality of life in terms of health, education, outlook.

The first lesson was that without the active participation of the people the process of development would be both lopsided and short lived. What was achieved was possible even against great odds because unlike at present, a TISS graduate devoted his whole working life of 35 years in those villages knowing each one by name and their problems. This is essential if one has to mould the attitude and outlook of villagers. 'A grasshopper approach to this problem will be illusionary and deceptive'. 'Rural work is personally intensive and lack of devoted, efficient and honest field workers is a stumbling block,' says Mr. Suratwala. While providing all necessary guidance the NGOs should avoid excessive spoonfeeding. It should be clear to the villagers that the primary responsibilities for improving the conditions of living is in their hands. All the NGOs provide are technical inputs, finance or advice on obtaining finance and guidance. Those who have studied up to S.S.C. or who have a stake in the villages in terms of land or house should be associated with the planning and execution of development programmes.

A shortage of finance is not a serious hurdle in the way of rural development. A large chunk of the investments for this project from 1971-72 was obtained from government's own schemes which the villagers do not know about, be it to excavate or deepen a well, instal a pump, purchase bullock or fertilisers.

Material incentives do have a selective and limited role only. A certain degree of idealism on the part of the social worker, a liking for rural environment and a sincere desire to work for the backward communities are also called for. The Sir Dorabji Tata Trust rural work programme insisted on the sanctity of returning loans to co-operative societies, nationalised banks and other institutions which our Trust officials enabled them to obtain. A few years back the State Government suddenly decided to write off all arrears of debt up to a certain amount. Overnight thirty years of efforts to teach the farmers the sanctity of loans that he had taken for digging wells, buying electric motors, tractors, seeds and fertilisers at a low rate of interest was nullified.

The Devapur experiment showed that the Employment Guarantee Scheme, laudable in its objectives, not only increased the scope for corruption but encouraged laziness and created shortage of labour for essential seasonal operation on farms. The report notes that Family Planning was not at all the felt need of the people when the work began and as a consequence of the delay in introducing Family Planning a proportion of the economic development in Devapur was neutralised by the increase in population. As a follow-up to his 35 years of work S.R. Suratwala adds:

'When I first came to this God forsaken area there was much poverty. There was hardly a bicycle per village. Now every home has a bicycle and the standard of living has improved. But when I came there was a greater spirit of neighbourness, a desire to help at any time of night or day. Today that is much less. If rural work has to ultimately succeed, man too has to change.'

Chapter 17

From Central Asia to the Pacific

The first Institute for Population Studies in the developing world was a brainchild of Dr. John Matthai when he was Chairman of the Trust. The Institute was born on the premises of the Tata Institute of Social Sciences at Chembur. In December 1954, Dr. Matthai proposed to the Health Minister of India, Rajkumari Amrit Kaur, that a School of Population Studies be started in association with the Tata Institute of Social Sciences. Such a school, he felt, would train a nucleus of persons who would carry out population studies for the government or the universities. He also indicated that the UN may well be interested in participating in this venture if its facilities could be made available for this region of Asia.

The following year when Rajkumari Amrit Kaur was at the UN Conference in Europe, she discussed the matter with the UN officials, including Philip De Seynes, the then Under Secretary for Economic and Social Affairs at the UN. Officials of the UN were keenly interested in the proposal for the ECAFE region, which then extended from Afghanistan to the Philippines.

In July 1956, the Union Government approved of a joint undertaking with the Sir Dorabji Tata Trust for a Demographic Centre for Training and Research in which the UN would collaborate. The UN was to supply the expertise and meet some of the capital expenditure, the Union Government was to meet a large part of the recurring expenses, and the Dorabji Tata Trust was to meet one-sixth of the cost of running the Centre for five consecutive years.

Till premises for the Demographic Centre were erected, it was housed at the Tata Institute of Social Sciences, the bungalow of the Director serving as its focal point, with students having access to TISS classes and library. The Demographic Centre, from the very beginning, was envisaged as an institute that would work on a cooperative basis with the TISS, the Gokhale Institute of Politics and Economics at Pune, the School of Economics and Sociology at the Bombay University and the Indian Cancer Research Centre, Bombay.

Land for the Institute was found at Chembur within a stone's throw of the TISS—a farm gifted by the Ratan Tata Trust. What is today a built-up area at the extremity of Bombay was then so wild that a couple of mongooses were adopted to take care of the snakes that abounded. From the start, the UN was generous in its fellowships, and pupils started flowing in from near and far, more recently, even from the Pacific islands. About 700 students have been trained to date, of whom about 300 have come from 24 foreign countries, including Indonesia, Afghanistan, Bangladesh, Iran, South Korea, the Philippines and the Republic of China.

The Institute has been fortunate in having distinguished men as its Directors, beginning with the former Director-General of Health, Dr. K.C.K.E. Raja, who was the Co-ordinating Officer of the Centre. The famous demographer, Dr. C. Chandrasekaran, was a Director. He was succeeded by Dr. K. Srinivasan, a distinguished statistician-demographer who has evaluated several projects, including family planning programmes in Sri Lanka and the Peoples' Republic of China. Its present officiating Director is Prof. (Ms.) Sumati Kulkarni.

When the Centre started, demography was not widely taught in India. Today it is part of the university studies in economics, statistics, sociology and geography. The scope of demography has widened and in July 1970 it was decided to change the name of the Demographic Training and Research Centre to International Institute for Population Studies. Having played its role in launching the institute under UN auspices and helped run it over 14 years, the Dorabji Tata Trust decided that its role as initiator and sponsor had been accomplished and its financial support was withdrawn in 1970. The success of this Institute has resulted in the opening of similar centres by the UN in Chile, Egypt, Ghana and the Cameroons.

The University Grants Commission has recommended that the International Institute of Population Studies be deemed a university.

The studies conducted at the Institute cover a wide range—'Fertility Decline in China' and 'Status of Women in Western Samoa', for example. As internal migration is becoming an important issue in India, the Institute has prepared a map of India's resources and population geography to help identify areas of resettlement. Apart from enriching knowledge of demography, the wider purpose of the Institute is to bring about through research, an improvement in the quality of life of the entire region, from Central Asia to the Pacific.

Chapter 18

A Multi-purpose Trust

In 1944, the then Chief Justice of India, Sir Maurice Gwyer, recommended to the Chairman, J.R.D. Tata, the case of a brilliant student, coming from the scheduled caste in Travancore, who had stood first class first at the B.A. Exam of the Madras University. The young man's name was K.R. Narayanan and he wanted to study further at the London School of Economics.

Not only did the J.N. Tata Endowment for Higher Education assist with a loan, but the Sir Dorabji Tata Trust and the Sir Ratan Tata Trust joined with larger grants that were substantial for that time to enable the young man to study abroad.* Circumstances, however, did not favour him. 'Those were the days of war and there was no ship so I was stranded here (Bombay)' said Narayanan at a Convocation of the TISS in 1995.

He had nowhere to stay, so Mrs. Pilloo Vesugar, Director of the J.N. Tata Endowment, requested Dr. J.M. Kumarappa, Director of the Tata Institute of Social Sciences, to allow him to stay in the hostel of the Institute, then situated at the Nagpada House, Bombay. 'Thus I stayed there nearly for one year in 1944-45. I was a journalist, a reporter in *The Times of India* at the same time and I came to know the students of the Institute, Prof. M.S. Gore, Mr. P.D. Kulkarni, Prof. Panakal, Mrs. Philis Gore all of them were friends and I have the privilege of keeping up the contact and friendship with them ever since. I must have acquired a basic inclination towards social work because I happened to marry someone later on who was also a social worker. In a sense I was or I have been a perpetual object of compassionate social work in my life. In any case the stay at Nagpada house enabled

---

*A total of over Rs.17,000/-, equivalent to Rs.5.85 lakhs of today.

me to pick up smatterings of the knowledge of social work and social science which stood me in good stead in the London School of Economics and later in life.'

After he went abroad, the J.N. Tata Endowment for Higher Education kept a close watch on his career at the London School of Economics where he read Politics and Economics. A J.N. Tata Endowment's noting from the records of February 12, 1946 reads 'Excellent progress'. The report of May 6, 1946 reads 'Very satisfactory'. One of his mark-sheets read: British Constitution 75%, Economic History 70%, Logic 60%. The entry of July 1947 reads 'passed out First Class'.

For his return to India, Narayanan's professor at the London School of Economics, Harold Laski gave a personal letter recommending him to Prime Minister Jawaharlal Nehru. Nehru appointed him in the External Affairs Ministry as an Attache. While he was second secretary of the Indian High Commission in erstwhile Burma, Narayanan received a letter from a Ma Tint Tint, then teaching at Rangoon University, to deliver a lecture on Human Rights organised under the auspices of the United Nations. The *Indian Express* observes 'that letter brought two loving hearts together' and resulted in K.R. Narayanan's marriage to the young Burmese lady, now called Usha Narayanan. After a distinguished career as Ambassador to China and the U.S.A., K.R. Narayanan was elected as Vice-President of India in 1992 and in 1997 President of India.

Relief of Distress

Sir Dorabji had made special mention in his Trust Deed of the relief of distress and the first allocation was for flood relief in Cuttack and Puri in December 1933. Then came relief for the victims of the Bihar and Quetta earthquakes, and the 'immediate relief of famine stricken Bhils of Dohad Taluka'. A modest allocation was made in 1935 to Dr. B.R. Ambedkar for the reconstruction of huts destroyed by fire in the area of Amboli. In November 1939, allocations were made for the Polish Refugees Fund in London and the National Red Cross Society of China in Hong Kong.

On the attainment of Independence, in 1947, Jawaharlal Nehru started the Prime Minister's National Relief Fund. On the Board of Trustees in 1962 there were five members: the Prime Minister, the President of the Indian National Congress, the Minister for Finance, a representative of the Tata Trusts (P.A. Narielwala) and a representative of the Federation of the Indian Chambers of Commerce and Industry.

Under the auspices of the Sir Dorabji Tata Trust, the Tata Relief Committee, a permanent body available to rush assistance to distress-hit areas was formed. The Tata Companies and Trusts move in concert to assist. At the time of the Andhra cyclone in 1977, it constructed 600 houses and 11 special community centres on stilts to provide refuge if a cyclone struck again. The design of the centres was taken from the Philippines which frequently experiences cyclones. These community centres served as schools or dispensaries in normal times but were designed to provide shelter for 1,200 persons in an emergency.

In May 1979 the dreaded event took place again. The same areas were struck by a second cyclone. Thanks to

earlier warnings the villagers in the area of Repalle and Avanigadda rushed to the Tata-built community centres. They shook as they witnessed, through the windows of the centre, telephone and telegraph poles torn apart and houses built by other agencies being razed. A cyclone of high intensity hit the same district of coastal Andhra Pradesh again in 1990 sweeping aside entire villages. Tata Relief officials awaited news of whether their community centres had withstood the fury. The *Indian Express* reported on May 10, 1990 'the cyclone shelters built after the 1977 cyclone have come in handy to house the evacuated people from low lying areas of the coastal districts.' They had withstood the test of the cyclone fury.

After the Latur earthquake Tata Companies contributed Rs. 4.83 crores for relief. Four hundred and two houses were built in two villages, plus the roads and the community buildings. The creditable part is the workers' unions take the initiative often and the Company's Board matches it. Tata Steel workers collected Rs. 1 crore and the Management matched their contribution. They spared two of their Engineers to assist Tata Housing who set up the houses. The Trust co-ordinated it as it has when calamities strike like the Panshet Dam disaster and the Koyna earthquake. The expertise of Tata Consulting Engineers and other companies could be called upon.

Tata Consulting Engineers incorporated within the Government design earthquake-proof features used for nuclear power reactors when constructed to secure them from any risk in a future earthquake.

*　　　*　　　*

Integrated Development

The Trust had been engaged in a programme of sinking of wells for drinking water or other specific needs but has increasingly moved to an integrated development with a wider range of services.

In May 1981, a letter came to the Trust from P.D. Karandikar, Collector of Sholapur, Maharashtra. 'I am writing this letter,' he wrote, 'to express my sincere gratitude for the work of drilling programme carried out on behalf of Sir Dorabji Tata Trust, Bombay, by Sholapur Well Service for ten villages. I am also thankful for your decision to take up the programme in twenty more villages.' The Collector requested that the Trust consider stepping up the programme to 'at least 100 bore wells'. While the Trust hesitated to plunge into the programme immediately, at its bi-annual meeting in August 1981, it did sanction a further programme, bringing the total there to 45 wells. In addition, 45 wells were sanctioned for the Maan Taluka, Maharashtra, and for the Panchmahal District in Gujarat. Borings have also been sponsored by the Trust in drought prone areas of Rajasthan.

In 1940, long before adivasi welfare work became popular, B.G. Kher, a former Premier of Bombay Presidency had, with the blessings of Gandhiji, started the Adivasi Seva Mandal. It sought to create, among the three lakh adivasis of Thane District, a consciousness about their rights. Their lot was pitiable. They were in the grip of money-lenders, of landlords and of drink. To educate them and lift them up was a considerable undertaking. From 1946 to 1972 the Trust steadily supported the Mandal with a small grant.

*   *   *

In more recent years one of the priority areas of the Trust is in the field of sustainable development. Micro industries like micro water projects not only cost less but often go much further in their impact. A lady in Andhra Pradesh was given Rs. 500 by an NGO to open a tea shop in her home on the road side. She employed one person, then two persons, and then finally her husband. Her economic independence not only resulted in her family being looked after but heightened her social status.

The finding of the Trust is that women are most dependable when they take loans. The benefit of what they earn also goes far more to the family than in the case of men. In Andhra and in Bihar the Trust has concentrated on micro industries. In other places like Gujarat the Trust has concentrated on integrated development including education, judicial knowledge and women rights in places like Kutch which has the highest suicide rate for women. This concern of the Trust to give dignity to the women of India is as Prof. Arthur E. Hold put it to the first group of TISS students 'is not a hundred yard dash; it is a long distance championship'. Similarly for water projects, giving funds for bore wells is not the answer as the water table is getting lower in most parts of India. The early lessons of the Trust in Devapur of preserving water through bund building on ..... and small bunds across rivers is more relevant today. The Trust has to adapt this technique to the needs of society which have been aggravated by the population explosion.

Advancement of Learning

Universities have over the years been recipients of grants from the Dorabji Tata Trust. The Bombay University received a grant (on the occasion of its centenary in 1958) as also the SNDT Women's University, Bombay, and the Gokhale Institute of Politics and Economics, Pune, primarily for a department of agricultural economics. The National Chemical Laboratory, Pune, received a grant at its inception.

Literary and cultural organisations like the Asiatic Society, Bombay; the Tagore Society, Jamshedpur; and the Indian Council of World Affairs, Bombay Branch, each received grants. Back in 1934, Dr. Rabindranath Tagore had received a modest grant for Shantiniketan.

A number of artistes, musicians and dancers have been recipients of grants. The late Neville Chinoy, the child prodigy pianist, received a grant for higher studies, so did the dancer Indrani Rehman. Mehli Mehta, father of the conductor Zubin Mehta, was given a grant in March 1945 to go to the United States 'to attain virtuosity and to get training in conducting at the Curtiss Institute of Music, Philadelphia'. Thousands of students have received fellowships and scholarships. In 1934, C.V. Narasimhan was helped to proceed to Oxford for higher education. In later years he became the Deputy Secretary-General of the United Nations.

In 1996 a substantial grant of Rs. 5 crores was sanctioned by Sir Dorabji Tata Trust to enable the J.N. Tata Endowment to raise its loan amount to at least Rs. 100,000 each to over 100 selected students for studies abroad. In addition, a further Rs. 2 crores was donated to Jamsetji Tata Trust to give a grant component up to Rs. 100,000 to each of these students. In special cases, like that of twin brothers, both suffering from muscular dystrophy, going to study in the US, a supplementary grant is given by Sir Dorabji Tata Trust. But the main vehicle of Tatas for higher studies is the J.N. Tata Endowment for Higher Education.

In 1959, the centenary of the birth of Sir Dorabji Tata, the scheme was set in motion to encourage outstanding talent in eight Mumbai colleges. The student is given a stipend or a book prize depending upon the income of his family. The scheme now extended to 9 colleges is framed to request principals of the colleges concerned to send four of their promising students from the XII standard for an interview each year. A panel of educationists — the current chairman of the panel being Prof. R.R. Sahuraja, Principal of Podar College and Trust officers select about 12 to 16 scholars after an interview and a debate or a discussion. The student is given the Award until he or she gets the first degree. If it is a case of medical or engineering student, he or she will get the scholarship for as many as six years. Many of those who have been selected as the Sir Dorabji Tata Trust Merit Scholars later go abroad and qualify for higher positions in India or abroad.

Occasionally, on compassionate grounds, a scholarship is considered. One such was the case of 17-year old Nisarahmed Shaikh, son of a vegetable vendor of Jogeshwari, who had just entered college. From 4.30 each morning he would hawk vegetables until his father relieved him at 10.30 a.m. Then

Nisar went to college. Asked what he aspired to do on passing, Nisar replied, 'I would like to be a teacher'. 'You know how badly teachers are paid,' he was told. 'You are quite right,' he replied, 'but do you know how badly we are taught? That is why it is necessary that someone should make a sacrifice.' Sadly, Nisar's results may not have been good for he failed to turn up for his scholarship renewal. Efforts by the Trust to track him down failed. Perhaps if he reads these lines, he will know he is still remembered.

*   *   *

Sir Dorabji Tata Memorial Lectures

The Trustees felt the need for occasional intellectual stimulus that can come from special lectures by distinguished personalities in various fields of knowledge. Thus the Sir Dorabji Tata Memorial Lectures were instituted in 1959 on the occasion of the birth centenary of Sir Dorabji Tata. Those delivered so far are:

1960 Sir Oliver (later Lord) Franks, diplomat, banker, scholar: *Some Reflections on Monetary Policy*

1961 Lord Morrison, Deputy Prime Minister of the U.K.: *British Parliamentary Democracy*

1971 Mr. J.C. Shah, former Chief Justice of India: *The Rule of Law and the Indian Constitution*

1971 Dr. C.A. Doxiadis, Greek architect and urbanist: *Human Settlements*

1973 Sir Arthur Lewis (later awarded the Nobel Prize for Economics in 1979): *Dynamic Factors in Economic Growth*

1975 Dr. S. Dillon Ripley, Secretary, Smithsonian Institution: *The Paradox of the Human Condition*

1981 Ambassador Elliot L. Richardson, former Attorney General, USA: *The Uses and Limitations of Law*

1984 Sir George Porter, F.R.S., Director, The Royal Institution, London, Winner Nobel Prize for Chemistry

1967, *Science and Power — A View from 1984*
1990 Mr. Bernard Levin, eminent British journalist and author, *Utopia: The Eternal Dream and Responsibility Today*
1991-92 Sir John Thomson, British High Commissioner to India from 1977 to 1982, *The Population Explosion — Opportunity or disaster, The Migration Question — What is to be done about it?* and *Independent Sector — The saviour of Democratic Societies*
1995 Dr. Henry A. Kissinger, former U.S.A. Secretary of State and Nobel Peace Prize Winner in 1973, *International Policy after the Cold War*

These lectures are usually published and, like the BBC Reith Lectures make a contribution to original thinking.

*   *   *

Homi Bhabha Fellowship Scheme

Sir John Cockcroft, FRS and Nobel Laureate said at the Royal Institute in London:

> Human progress has always depended on the achievements of a few individuals of outstanding ability and creativeness. Homi Bhabha was one of those.

To enable such talent and creativity to blossom the Dorabji Tata Trust instituted a fellowship scheme in Dr. Homi Bhabha's name.

The Fellowships were awarded to persons between the ages of 25 and 38, when human energy and inventiveness are at their peak. As many are engaged in a career for a living, a person at that age often forgoes the pursuit of study or research for want of financial support. Such persons may have outstanding qualities of leadership in their field, but, little opportunity to exercise it. To search out and encourage such exceptional talent in varied fields of the arts, industry, agriculture, commerce and social organisation, the Homi

Bhabha Fellowships Council was started at the initiative of the Trust in 1966. The Ford Foundation joined in from the outset to provide both generous assistance and the foreign exchange equivalent of the Fellowships required to supplement study, research and travel abroad. Many a Fellow was unknown at the time of selection but, within a few years, has gained recognition. There is Shyam Benegal, the film director; Girish Karnad, playwright and actor; and Arun Shourie, winner of the Magsaysay Award for journalism, wrote a study entitled, 'Statistical Technique in Economics'. Mr. Darryl D'Monte pursued his interest in the field of environment. It is not mandatory for them to produce a book but many of them do.

One Fellow studied the history of Mughal architecture; a second did research in cardiology; a third, into the 'Planning and Development of New Towns'; and a fourth made a 'Search for a New Identity in the Tribal Communities of Orissa'. A person can be recommended by an institution or even by an eminent person in his field of endeavour. Mrs. Nelly Sethna, concerned about the 'Dying Textile Crafts of India', made a study of the problem and recommended ways to keep the craft alive.

Family Planning and Health

J.R.D. Tata was among the very first to warn Jawaharlal Nehru that India's plans would run into difficulties with the exploding population. During the Independence struggle it was believed that India's population was her strength, and far from accepting Mr. Tata's note of caution, Prime Minister Nehru said that her population was India's asset. In 1970, Mr. Tata helped to found, with other industrialists and public men, the Family Planning Foundation in New Delhi. To that Foundation the Dorabji Tata Trust contributed generously. It also supports other ventures connected with population control. It helped in making available some facilities at the

Institute for Research in Reproduction which studies various aspects of fertility control. Since then, bodies which concentrate on assisting women, like the Strihitakarini working in the slums of Mumbai have also received assistance.

Minority Institutions

Minority institutions are not forgotten. In June 1963, A.A. Peerbhoy, Head of the Anjuman-I-Islam, wrote to the Managing Trustee: 'The Tata Trust has been a source of great encouragement and strength to the Anjuman for a very long time.' Way back in the 1930s and mid-1940s grants were made for a girls' high school and a commerce high school through M.A. Jinnah, who had made the request.

Among the Mughal ruins in Aurangabad called Rauza Bagh, the Maulana Azad Education Society has set up a number of institutions. 'After 300 years Rauza Bagh has sprung to new life,' says an observer. 'Once again the air is redolent of roses, jasmines and the queen of the night. The old Madrasa now bustles with activity. Where Peer Ismail taught Arabic and Persian and the sacred law of the Quran and Hadith to the sons of the aristocracy, over 1,500 boys and girls of all classes, communities and castes are now taught modern languages, science and technology.' Among other objectives, the institution seeks to integrate more closely the Marathi and Urdu speaking elements of the population. The Society received a grant as it started off on its mission.

*   *   *

Handicapped

The Trust has encouraged institutions advancing the cause of the deaf, the blind, and the disabled. The Central Society of Education of the Deaf, and the Audiology and Research Centre, have received assistance. Often the allocations are for specific projects. Institutions that serve ex-Servicemen or serving officers receive special consideration.

Part VII

IN THE LIVES OF

THE PEOPLE

Chapter 19

The Ultimate Test

Establishing large institutions is a pride of a Trust but the ultimate test is what happens in the lives of the people not only through these institutions but in the day-to-day operations of the Trust. Modern philanthropy, originating in the West, prefers to concentrate on a few select areas of operation. It makes the task of both, administration and monitoring much easier. We have much to learn from it. There is however a world beyond it especially in a country where there is no social security assured by the Government. When the head of a major Western foundation heard that the Sir Dorabji Tata Trust gave individual grants for about a thousand individuals a year, to meet part of their cost towards a heart or a kidney surgery or cancer treatment and other ailments, he said, quite moved, 'We are bloodless.'

It has been the distinctive characteristic of the Sir Dorabji Tata Trust, thanks to the tradition established by its earlier wise leadership, that it has borne this human aspect in mind. The smallest grant one year was for Rs. 125/- for a pair of spectacles for a poor man who could not get it otherwise. To this man a pair of specs made all the difference between functioning or not functioning in life. Often the effort to undertake such an investigation is the same as that for spending 100 times that amount. It is gratifying to receive letters from people after recovering.

Over the years the Trust has, as we have seen, aided institutions for the physically handicapped and the mentally retarded, institutions for victims of leprosy, and for the care of the blind, and the training of teachers for the blind and the deaf. The list is long. But perhaps the most moving contributions are listed under the medical head. Scores of patients going in for kidney transplants, or bone marrow, heart surgery and cancer treatment, have received aid. The

sums needed for treatment in India or abroad are considerable and can go up to Rs. 24 lakhs or more. Any grant that the Trust makes is nominal compared to the total needs, but it may help to release the purse-strings of many other Trusts and individuals in India.

In 1977, the Trust received a letter from a Major Vijay Bhatnagar for assistance in having a kidney transplant in the USA. 'This is an appeal to you,' the letter said, 'to save a family. Major Vijay Bhatnagar, 36 years of age is married and has two small children....' A grant of a few thousand rupees was made. Major Bhatnagar had a successful operation and three years later the Trust received a letter from his wife stating that they had started the Major Vijay Bhatnagar Kidney Foundation in Jaipur to help patients who needed assistance for renal complaints. 'Should you come across a patient suffering from renal failure, you can refer him to us for information, guidance, contacts in India or abroad, as well as financial support,' wrote Mrs. Asha Bhatnagar, who organises campaigns to raise money for others in need. Philanthropy can at times trigger off a chain reaction.

Some of the experienced staff at the Dorabji Tata Trust also assist those in need with advice on where they should apply for further help and with their vast experience even indicate the most economic places to have heart, kidney or bone marrow operations in the West where essential but India is quite advanced enough. At times the Trust does not wait for appeals to come in. *The Times of India* of January 14, 1979, carried the news that Miss Farida Tayabee Bengali, 18, first year B.Com. student, needed a heart valve replacement. Dr. Denton Cooley of Houston, Texas, had agreed to do the operation and waive his professional fees. The Trust office read the news item, contacted the family and made a token contribution.

Some remember to keep in touch months or even years later. Mr. Suresh V. Desai of Raigad District, Maharashtra, wrote on the first anniversary of the successful operation of his son at a Harley Street clinic for a congenital heart complaint:

While we celebrate today the first anniversary of this event which ended our mental agony and brought back happiness, mental peace to our family, we remember you very much for the helping hand extended by you at a very crucial time in our family, without which perhaps, we would not have been able to have our son with us today. We are ever grateful to you.

Rajesh Singha was a blind M.A. student at St. Stephen's, Delhi. His request for help to study at the University of Cincinnati reached Sir Dorabji Tata Trust. He wanted to specialise in Modern American Drama. Rajesh was the first blind person to have received a television contract from Delhi Doordarshan. He played the violin and interviewed distinguished personalities. He had a small scholarship from the US university but needed supplementary help which the Trust provided on compassionate grounds. After some months the then Director of the Trust, D.K. Malegamvala, received a letter to say:

> You will be pleased to learn that one of the retinal specialists here has performed an operation that has been an amazing success. I am now able to see large letters and read ordinary print when enlarged. I have seen things in my immediate surroundings the existence of which I wasn't even aware of. The reactions of my parents knew no bounds when they learnt of the success of my eye operation.

The Trusts real contribution is etched in the lives of people—a patient at the Tata Memorial who has recovered; a villager who rejoices at the first sight of drinking water in his village; the excitement of a radio-astronomer as a new pulsar comes within his ken; the thrill of a mountaineer standing atop a Himalayan peak; or the quiet thanksgiving of a mother whose child, after heart surgery, first opens his eyes and recognises her face.

The ultimate test of any philanthropy is what happens in the lives of people. If today someone somewhere is walking, is seeing, or is healthy with a pace-maker ticking away, it is because of the grace of the Creator and because of the vision of an old man of 72 who left all his wealth in a Trust that has been managed with care and consideration for over sixty years. Was it Tolstoy who said:

> Not till here and there, one is thinking of us, one is loving us, does this waste earth become a peopled garden.

Epilogue

Finance is not the only way a Trust can serve the nation and its people. A Trust, intelligently managed, can become a catalyst that brings together other institutions and people. The Trust provides the necessary ideas and initiatives required. In the 1980s Sir Dorabji Tata Trust observed that while large Trusts like the Sir Dorabji Tata Trust had the finest legal and financial advice in the country (one of its senior Trustees is the eminent tax expert, N.A. Palkhivala), medium-sized and smaller Trusts were less fortunate. Instead of doing their essential work of helping good causes they had to spend their time going through a plethora of laws and regulations which sometimes conflicted with each other. For example, in the mid-80s the Charity Commissioner of Maharashtra ruled that Trusts (earlier prohibited), could thereafter invest in specified debentures. At the end of the financial year the Income Tax announced that any securities so held would make the Trust liable for income tax on its *entire* annual income. There was no organisation to guide the charities nor any equivalent of a Chamber of Commerce that could represent their case before the State and Central Governments.

The Trust after discussing the issue with some leading personalities in the field of philanthropy called a meeting at Bombay House (the Headquarters of Tatas) and as a result of the deliberations the proposal to start a Centre for Advancement of Philanthropy was accepted. Such a Centre could advise charities on taxation and other laws on charity, assisting those who wished to start to draft their Trust deed, register duly, obtain the necessary tax certificate, and help with their day-to-day problems. The Centre also undertook to hold seminars to train people including NGOs in the field of philanthropy.

The launching of the Centre would have been difficult without the co-operation of a recently retired Commissioner of Income-Tax (Trust Circle), R.R. Chari, who since its inception in 1986 till the date of writing of this epilogue has kindly given his honorary and expert services to the Centre and to hundreds of Trusts.

The first Chairman of the Centre was Mr. H.T. Parekh, Chairman of H.D.F.C. (Housing Development Finance Corporation). To begin with the Centre started India's first magazine entirely devoted to philanthropy with information on laws and other information relevant to philanthropic work. It is to date the only magazine of its kind. The Centre has published four handbooks written by its Executive Secretary, Noshir Dadrawala:

1. Handbook on Administration of Trusts
2. The Art of Fund Raising
3. Investment Opportunities for Charitable Organisations
4. Management of Philanthropic Organisations.

The Centre has organised training courses and has earned the appreciation not only of those engaged in the work of philanthropy but of officials like Justice K.M. Desai, who as Charity Commissioner of Maharashtra, wrote: 'I am a regular reader of the magazine "Philanthropy" being published by the Centre for Advancement of Philanthropy.* For all the philanthropists in Mumbai, it will act as good guidance. I am already talking to other persons about the work being put in by the Centre for Advancement of Philanthropy.' Speaking of its publications he observes: 'What we need in India today, is such type of simple publications, giving to the common man an insight in different laws, which do govern our day-to-day activities . . . all such publications do help to wipe out judicial illiteracy in our society.'

On retirement Justice Desai joined the Board of Directors of the Centre for Advancement of Philanthropy.

Other Trusts and philanthropically inclined companies have supported the Centre. Its track record of service of over a

---

* Centre for Advancement of Philanthropy, c/o Forbes Marshall, Mistry Mansion, 4th Floor, 107, M.G. Road, Mumbai 400 023.

decade has earned it the appreciation of the philanthropic community

*   *   *

Another initiative of the Trust was born as a result of a speech that the late Prime Minister Rajiv Gandhi made on the occasion of the Golden Jubilee of the Tata Institute of Social Sciences (TISS) in 1986. Looking ahead to the next 50 years Mr. Gandhi said that the emerging problems that needed to be tackled by social scientists lay in the arena of drug addiction, elevating the condition of women and protecting the environment.

He was keen that India got a grip on drug addiction before it assumed the alarming proportions that it had in some countries of the West. The very next day after the Prime Minister's visit the Trustees started planning how the first objective of the Prime Minister could be implemented. As a result a Drug Abuse Action Group was formed and meetings were held by the Trust inviting a cross section of those already involved in the drug action field. The Trust found· that those who engaged in this field had hardly ever come together and sometimes even officials of State Government and the Municipal Corporation were working on parallel lines, one not knowing what the other was planning to do. From the beginning the Police Chief in charge of Narcotics was included in the Action Group.

During the very first meeting, the Drug Action Group noted that drug addiction was a specialised field and the ordinary medical practitioner did not feel himself competent to deal with the problem. So the Trust proposed that a Directory of Information in the field of Substance Abuse— Drugs and Alcohol was essential, as to where an addict could go for detoxification and where he could be rehabilitated. Work on the Directory was undertaken and a reference book published by the TISS. The next initiative was a telephone 'Helpline' that drug addicts and their families could turn to. The Kripa Foundation responded to take on manning a telephone 'Helpline', financially undergirded by the Trust in its early years of operation.

Fr. Joe Pereira, Director of the Kripa Foundation says that 'The Action Group played an important role in the fight against drug abuse providing for the first time a common meeting place for various persons and institutions working in the field of drug abuse. The most significant contribution is the opportunity given to people genuinely working in the field of drug abuse to both assess the work as well as focus attention on issues that would promote healthy growth of the organisations involved in the work.'

When this work grew, the Trust requested the TISS to look after it.

Short courses or seminars for the training of social workers engaged in helping drug and alcohol addicts have been held. Perhaps a regular course for which diplomas could be awarded may be the next step.

*   *   *

In 1946, two lady pioneers of family planning started their quiet work at K.E.M. Hospital, Pune. One was Ms. Shakuntala Paranjpe; the other a young doctor who had just joined the K.E.M., Dr. Banoobai Coyaji.

In 1951 the first national figure to call for Family Planning was J.R.D. Tata. On the eve of India's First Five Year Plan being launched he foresaw that India's planning benefits would be nullified or watered down if her population was not checked. With remarkable consistency he repeated his views and in 1970 started the Family Planning Foundation of India (later called The Population Foundation) in conjunction with the Ford Foundation and contributions from some Tata Companies, Trusts and the support of a few far-sighted industrialists. In recognition of his consistent efforts over 40 years, J.R.D. Tata was given the U.N. Population Award in 1992. Earlier the same year the President of India Mr. Venkataraman conferred on Mr. Tata the nation's highest civilian award, the Bharat Ratna. The President told this writer that he had in mind the social contributions of Mr. Tata, like Family Planning, when he thought of conferring the Bharat Ratna on him. As Chairman of the Population Foundation, J.R.D. Tata had invited Dr. Banoobai Coyaji to join the Board.

Dr. Banoobai Coyaji gained international recognition with her work for the rural women of India. For 12 years she was on the Scientific and Technical Advisory Group (STAG) of the W.H.O. She visited 120 countries, processing their appeals for grants for the welfare of women and children. She established two remarkable projects outside Pune running several primary health centres and two rural hospitals in the catchment area of the hospital that she headed — the K.E.M. Hospital in Pune. Thereby she reduced the flow of the rural people to Pune's hospitals with minor complaints taking medical facilities nearer to their homes. The Magsaysay Award was primarily bestowed on her for this work.

As J.R.D. Tata was Chairman of Sir Dorabji Tata Trust, a couple of years after his death, Dr. Banoobai Coyaji wrote an appeal to the Trustees. Looking back over 50 years Dr. Coyaji wrote, 'The important mistake we all made was only to concentrate on family planning. More or less the same will not do for the 90s and beyond. The quality of service must improve considerably.'

She submitted her plan for a comprehensive family planning centre which included reproductive health services for adolescents; a separate male family planning clinic which would include sex health education, treatment of sexual dysfunction, informed choice of family planning methods and prevention of sexually transmitted diseases—all under one roof with experts. She recognised that man was an important factor in family planning and needed help, and should have a place to come to.

She offered a 4,000 sq. ft. flat, formerly her own quarters as Director of K.E.M., as the place to start the Centre. Therefore, there was no expenditure on 'brick and mortar' except for renovations.

Her nine-point programme includes:

1. Prevention and management of unwanted pregnancy.
2. Diagnosis and treatment of infertility and unsuccessful pregnancy, i.e. repeated abortions, foetal death and still births.
3. Prevention and treatment of reproductive tract infections and sexually transmitted infections.
4. Sexual health, gender information and counselling.
5. Reproductive health services for adolescents.
6. Safe motherhood and child survival services.
7. Prevention and referral of gynaecological problems.
8. Screening, early diagnosis and referral of breast and cervical cancer of the reproductive tract.
9. Setting up a separate Male Family Planning clinic.

Under one roof will be facilities for sex health education, diagnosis and treatment of sexual dysfunction, infertility counselling, informed choice of Family Planning methods, prevention of STDs and HIV, treatment of STD, etc.

The Trustees sanctioned her a grant of Rs. 80 lakhs for the programme. She made a final request. In view of J.R.D. Tata's interest in the subject could she get permission to name it after J.R.D. Tata. The request was conceded.

*   *   *

In 1964 a young doctor, M.H. Keswani, was helped to go to England by the Trust for specialisation in plastic surgery and to assist with the Tata Department for Plastic Surgery, at the J.J. Hospital, Mumbai. The young man returned from England and specialised in the treatment of burns. He was one of the founders of the Burns Association of India and with creditable devotion for 30 years organised courses in burns treatment for doctors and nurses throughout India sometimes supported by the Trust. Often he invited experts from abroad to take workshops. He put before the Trust his proposal to start on his long-standing dream of an Institute for the Research, Education and Treatment of Burns. The climatic conditions of India are not quite conducive to the western treatment of burns. India's ancient Shastras have mentioned formulas for the treatment of burns. Further research needs to be conducted to marry our ancient wisdom with up-to-date methods. In 1995 he came to the Trustees with his plans to start the Institute and the Trustees sanctioned a substantial grant as seed money for this pioneering enterprise.

*　　*　　*

It is much easier to manage a Trust keeping in mind just four or five priorities, shutting out the rest of human needs. So far, the Sir Dorabji Tata Trust has kept its windows open to a wide variety of needs as its Trust objectives, wisely framed, instructed it to do.

A trust of some magnitude has to keep its antenna sensitive to what needs arise in society, and at the right moment — preferably when the right person is found — to move in it with its resources and experience.

*　　*　　*

An Institute for Tropical Diseases

A Trust to be effective needs to be faithful to its past, sensitive to the present and hopeful for the future.

The Indian Institute of Science, Bangalore, which was conceived by Jamsetji Tata, came into being in 1911. In 1912 Sir Dorabji Tata proposed to the Director of this Institute a benefaction as large as his father's to start a School for Tropical Diseases at the Institute. Sir Dorabji stated that his father was interested in medical investigations and that was not being pursued at the Institute. The Institute had just commenced at that time with emphasis on disciplines of engineering and the Director was not keen to diversify into medical research at that time.

Sir Dorabji did not call off his pursuit for a School of Tropical Medicine and in 1920 he met personalities of the Royal Society of London and discussed with them the possibility of establishing it in Bombay. Although the Royal Society was willing to assist, somehow the proposal did not fructify.

In 1997, the Sir Dorabji Tata Trust returned to fulfil the desire of its Founder. In fact the need for research into these diseases is even more urgent today with the resurgence of diseases like malaria and T.B. and the additional burden of new diseases. After suitable explorations, it was decided that the Indian Institute of Science, Bangalore, was best suited.

Dr. V. Ramalingamswami, former Director-General of the Indian Council for Medical Research (ICMR) is adviser to the Trust on this project. In view of the Bangalore Institute's expertise in advanced biological sciences and the skills of its scientists, the Trustees decided to sanction a grant of Rs. 5 crores for the Sir Dorabji Tata Centre for Tropical and Emerging Tropical Diseases. Dr. Ramalingamswami has the conviction that this Institute will be a centre of knowledge to generate capability in molecular biology within the country and its research will be of considerable benefit to other developing countries.

APPENDICES

A. Chairmen of Sir Dorabji Tata Trust
B. Trustees of Sir Dorabji Tata Trust
C. Managing Trustees of Sir Dorabji Tata Trust
D. Directors and Secretaries of Sir Dorabji Tata Trust
E. Tata Institute of Social Sciences:
                    Chairmen/Directors
F. Tata Memorial Hospital/Centre:
                    Chairmen/Directors
G. Tata Institute of Fundamental Research:
                    Chairmen/Directors
H. National Centre for the Performing Arts:
                    Chairmen/Trustee-in-Charge/
                    Executive Directors
J. The Jubilee Diamond
K. Tata Institute of Fundamental Research —
A Summing Up

APPENDIX A

Sir Dorabji Tata Trust
Chairmen: 1932 – 1997

Sir Dorabji Tata	1932
Sir Nowroji Saklatvala	1932-1938
Sir Sorab Saklatvala	1938-1948
Sir Homi Mody	1948-1949
Sir Ardeshir Dalal	1949
Mr. J.R.D. Tata	1949-1950
Dr. John Matthai	1951-1957
Sir Homi Mody	1957-1969
Mr. J.R.D. Tata	1969-1993
Mr. R.N. Tata	1995-

APPENDIX B

Sir Dorabji Tata Trust
Trustees: 1997

1. Mr. R.N. Tata	*Chairman*
2. Mr. J.J. Bhabha	*Vice-Chairman & Managing Trustee*
3. Mr. N.A. Palkhivala	*Trustee*
4. Mr. P.L. Deshpande	*Trustee*
5. Dr. M.S. Swaminathan	*Trustee*
6. Dr. M.S. Gore	*Trustee*
7. Dr. F.A. Mehta	*Trustee*

APPENDIX C

Sir Dorabji Tata Trust
Managing Trustees

Prof. R.D. Choksi	1950-1980
Mr. J.J. Bhabha	1980-

APPENDIX D

Sir Dorabji Tata Trust
Directors / Secretaries

Dr. Clifford Manshardt	*Director*	1936-1941
Prof. R.D. Choksi	*Director*	1941-1950
Mr. D.S. Framroze	*Secretary*	1941-1954
Mr. S.K. Aiyar	*Secretary*	1955
Mr. N.D. Godbole	*Secretary*	1956-1962
Mr. R.D. Doongaji	*General Secretary*	1964-1971
Mr. G.K. Chandiramani	*Director*	1971-1977
Mr. D.K. Malegamvala	*Director*	1977-1985
Mr. P.S. Sadri	*Secretary*	1977-1985
Mr. R.M. Lala	*Director*	1985-
Mr. S.N. Batliwalla	*Secretary*	1991-

APPENDIX E

Tata Institute of Social Sciences
Chairmen of the Governing Board

Sir Nowroji Saklatvala	1936-1938
Sir Sorab Saklatvala	1938-1949
Sir Homi Mody	1949
Mr. N.H. Tata	1949-1951
Dr. John Matthai	1951-1956
Prof. R.D. Choksi	1957-1971
Mr. J.J. Bhabha	1971-1995
Mr. B.G. Deshmukh	1995-

Directors

Dr. Clifford Manshardt	1938-1941
Dr. J.M. Kumarappa	1941-1953
Prof. A.R. Wadia	1953-1962
Dr. M.S. Gore	1962-1982
Dr. (Miss) Armaity Desai	1983-1995
Prof. Partha N. Mukherji	1996-

APPENDIX F

Tata Memorial Hospital/Centre
Chairmen of the Governing Council

Sir Sorab Saklatvala	1941-1948
Sir Ardeshir Dalal	1949
Mr. N.H. Tata	1949-1957
Dr. John Matthai	1957-1959
Col. Jaswant Singh	1960
Lt. Col. V. Srinivasan	1960-1962
Dr. H.J. Bhabha	1962-1966
Mr. Dharma Vira	1966
Dr. Vikram A. Sarabhai	1966-1971
Dr. H.N. Sethna	1972-1983
Dr. Raja Ramanna	1983-1987
Dr. M.R. Srinivasan	1987-1990
Dr. P.K. Iyengar	1990-1993
Dr. R. Chidambaram	1993-

Directors

Dr. J.G. Paymaster	1967-1973
Dr. D.J. Jussawalla	1973-1980
Dr. P.B. Desai	1980-1995
Dr. R.S. Rao (TMH)	1992-1995
Dr. (Miss) K.A. Dinshaw	1997-

APPENDIX G

Tata Institute of Fundamental Research
Chairmen of the Council of Management

Sir Sorab Saklatvala	1945-1948
Sir Ardeshir Dalal	1949
Mr. J.R.D. Tata	1950-1993
Mr. J.J. Bhabha	1994-

Directors

Dr. Homi J. Bhabha	1945-1966
Prof. M.G.K. Menon	1966-1975
Dr. B.V. Sreekantan	1976-1987
Prof. Virendra Singh	1987-1997
Prof. S.S. Jha	1997-

APPENDIX H

National Centre for the Performing Arts
Chairmen

Mr. J.R.D. Tata	1966-1987
Mr. J.J. Bhabha	1987-

Trustee-in-Charge

Mr. J.J. Bhabha	1966-1987

Executive Directors

Dr. V.K. Narayana Menon	1968-1982
Mr. P.L. Deshpande	1984-1993
Mrs. Vijaya Mehta	1993-

APPENDIX J

The Jubilee Diamond

The 245.35 carat Jubilee Diamond ranks as one of the world's largest diamonds, more than twice as large as the Koh-i-noor which is 108 carats. It was discovered in South Africa's famous Jagersfontein mine in 1895 and was first known as the Reitz diamond in honour of the President, F. W. Reitz of the Orange Free State. The stone was cut in 1897, the year Queen Victoria celebrated her diamond jubilee. Hence it was called the Jubilee Diamond.

A book on *Diamonds: Famous, Notable and Unique*[1] speaks of the 'cushion-shaped, brilliant-cut diamond of unsurpassed colour, clarity, brilliance and symmetry—a diamond so perfectly proportioned, it can be balanced on its culet which is less than 2 mm in diameter!'

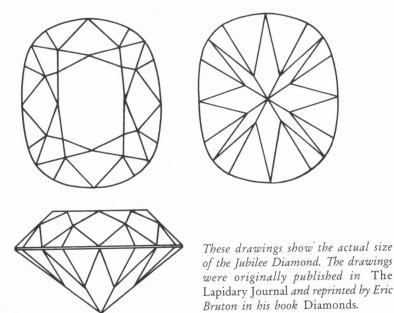

These drawings show the actual size of the Jubilee Diamond. The drawings were originally published in The Lapidary Journal *and reprinted by Eric Bruton in his book* Diamonds.

---

1 Published by the Gemmological Institute of America.

According to Eric Bruton, F.G.A. author of another book *Diamonds*[2], 'The Jubilee was exhibited at the Paris Exposition of 1900, where it received world-wide attention and the high praise of gem experts. Shortly thereafter, it was sold to Sir Dorabji Tata, a Parsi of Bombay and the founder of the Indian iron and steel industry, who owned it until his death. In 1939[3] the executors of Tata's estate sold the stone through Cartier Ltd., London.'

Eric Bruton notes it came into the possession of a Mr. Harry Winston and was valued at £ 714,000. The owner Mr. Paul-Louis Weiller of Paris, permitted its exhibition at the Smithsonian Institute, Washington, in 1960.

---

2 NAG Press, London, second edition, 1978.
3 Sir Dorabji Tata Trust records show the year as 1937. The net receipt after commission to Cartier was £ 66,750. Sir Dorabji is reported to have paid for it £ 100,000 in 1900.

APPENDIX K

The TIFR — A Summing Up

Prof. Virendra Singh
Director, TIFR at its Golden Jubilee Celebrations, 1996

Initially the research work in the Institute was in the area of cosmic rays and high energy physics, theoretical physics and mathematics. These are the areas in which Dr. Bhabha had a direct interest having made significant contributions.

Cosmic Ray Physics Group was, by mid-fifties, one of the largest in the world. Using specially designed photographic emulsions the discovery of K-meson, a strange elementary particle, was reported from TIFR along with other groups such as of Powell at Bristol. Some of the earliest examples of associated production of strange particles were also reported from here.

The Institute also created a Balloon Facility at Hyderabad to develop techniques of scientific ballooning in order to carry nuclear emulsion stacks to very high stratospheric altitudes in order to study high energy cosmic ray interactions. This facility, which has been successfully operating for more than 30 years, has been greatly useful in the Institute's present work in X-ray astronomy and infrared astronomy programmes. It has also been used for atmospheric research by other agencies. It is one of the four such facilities in the world.

Deep underground experiments on muon intensities and angular distributions at various depths at Kolar Gold Mines, established the feasibility of studying neutrino interactions. The first neutrino interactions anywhere in the world were recorded from Kolar. Experiments to look for proton decay at Kolar was again the first dedicated set up to study the proton lifetime at the level of 10^{31} years.

Extensive air showers generated by cosmic rays are studied at Ooty and Kolar and give important results on characteristics of ultra high energy interactions. The TIFR also carries out work in PeV gamma ray astronomy from here. X-ray astronomy work at the Institute is carried out using satellites apart from balloons. Important work in TeV gamma ray astronomy is being carried out by the TIFR using ground based systems from Pachmarhi in Madhya Pradesh.

The observational astronomy at the Institute started in 1963 with the establishment of Radio Astronomy group and commissioning of Ooty radio telescope in the late sixties. Ooty radio telescope, with its axis parallel to earth's axis, was feasible only in India. Their observations using lunar occultation technique of some thousand radio galaxies and quasars have provided important evidence in favour of big bang cosmology. The indigenous design of Ooty radio telescope led to considerable development of know-how and expertise in the area of antenna design.

The Institute is also in the process of setting up a Giant Metrewave Radio Telescope as a national facility near Pune. It would be the largest of such telescopes at these wavelengths in the world. It is based on a novel antenna design evolved at the Institute itself. It should be capable of tackling problems such as the epoch of galaxy formation.

The high energy physicists at TIFR are involved in collaborative research at leading accelerator centres at CERN, Geneva and at Fermilab at Batavia, USA. Our scientists have been involved in the discovery of the fundamental particle 'top quark' at Fermilab. At CERN they have been responsible for determining the properties of the quanta Z^0 of the electroweak force. For nuclear physics the Institute has installed a 14 MeV pelletron accelerator and it does accelerator-based atomic physics jointly with the Bhabha Atomic Research Centre.

The experimental matter programme has developed into a very strong research group working on high temperature super-conductivity, magnetism of intermetallics, ferrites, amorphous semiconductors and optoelectronics using a wide variety of techniques available to the workers. Chemical Physics programmes are related to molecular biophysics, bioinorganic chemistry and chemical dynamics. The group also operates a national 500 Megahertz as well as a 600 Megahertz FT-NMR facility to study structure of biomolecules.

The Molecular Biology programme at the Institute started in the early sixties and its present activities are in the area of neurobiology, yeast glycolysis, gene regulation in fruit flies, and development of malarial parasites. The Institute is setting up a National Centre for Biological Sciences at Bangalore to nurture high level research in fundamental biology and its applications.

Apart from the observational work, TIFR has very strong theoretical groups in the areas of high energy physics, condensed matter physics, astrophysics, nuclear physics and they have made significant contributions.

The School of Mathematics has emerged as one of the important research centres in pure mathematics especially in the areas of algebra, algebraic geometry, lie groups and number theory.

TIFR's involvement in science education has been both formal and informal. We operate a flourishing graduate school for training students in research in both schools of Physics and Mathematics. Homi Bhabha Centre for Science Education of TIFR has now grown into a major centre conducting innovative programmes aimed at improving the quality of science education and at designing specific remedial measures for boosting the scholastic performance of students belonging to the weaker section of society. It is also undertaking research in cognitive aspects of education.

High level technical spin offs have resulted from the fundamental research activity at the Institute. I need not repeat about our contribution to India's atomic energy programme.

Electronics group of this Institute was the nucleus from which grew the Electronics Division of BARC and eventually the Electronics Corporation of India Ltd. The work on linear accelerator led to the development and manufacture of microwave components and devices, which could contribute in a big way in designing and supplying critical components and subsystems required by many national agencies. This group has now been formed into a separate autonomous organisation, SAMEER.

Institute scientists designed one of the earliest digital computer over three decades ago — the first one in India. The work at the Institute has resulted in the formation of an independent centre 'National Centre for Software Technology' (NCST). Presently the computer scientists are working on processing speech generation, speech and script recognition and abstract aspects of computer science.

We look forward to the future with confidence, built out of our achievements in the past, high hopes for the continued excellence at the international level, and a firm belief in our role in the building of our nation.